THE SONG OF THE FOREST

You can see more of my work at:
https://brianmeyer.DivergeISay.com/
https://instagram.com/artbybrianmeyer/
and contact me directly at brian@DivergeISay.com

Copyright ©2026 Diverge I Say, Brian Meyer

Published by Diverge I Say
Paperback Grayscale Edition ISBN: 979-8-9914906-6-5
Published as a grayscale edition with digitally clothed figures.

First Printing March 2026
Published by Diverge I Say
San Diego, CA (Hillcrest)

All rights reserved.

No part of this book may be reproduced or transmitted in any form or by any means, electronic or mechanical, without prior written permission of the author, except for review purposes.

Permission is hereby granted for the public human performance, recitation, and reading of the poems within this book, in whole or in part, including the recording and dissemination of such performances on digital platforms such as YouTube and similar social media outlets, provided that Proper attribution is given to the author and the book title is clearly stated or displayed.

This permission explicitly excludes the creation, distribution, or sale of a commercial audiobook (e.g., an "Audible book," podcast, or similar audio-only product) as a separate commercial work.

The moral right of the author has been asserted

No part of this book may be used or reproduced in any manner for the purpose of training artificial intelligence technologies or systems. In accordance with Article 4(3) of the Digital Single Market Directive 2019/790, Diverge I Say expressly reserves this work from the text and data mining exception.

Cover design, texts and illustrations: copyright © 2026 Brian Meyer

"The sun shines not on us but in us.
The rivers flow not past, but through us.
Thrilling, tingling, vibrating every fiber and cell
of the substance of our bodies,
making them glide and sing.
The trees wave and the flowers bloom
in our bodies as well as our souls,
and every bird song, wind song,
and tremendous storm song
of the rocks in the heart of the mountains
is our song, our very own, and sings our love."

–John Muir

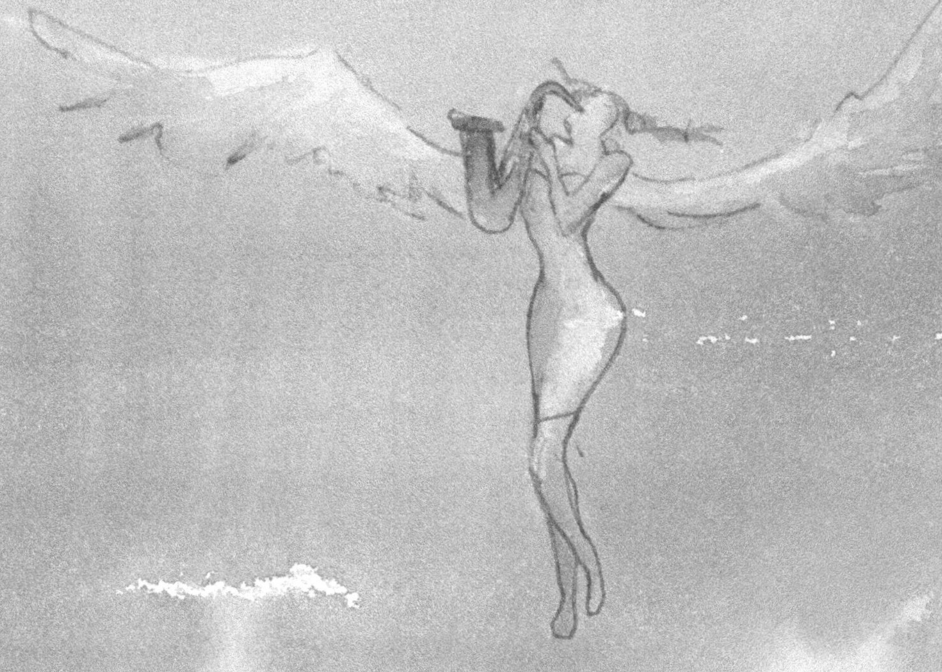

"I am a forest, and a night of dark trees:
but he who is not afraid of my darkness,
will find banks full of roses
under my cypresses."

–Friedrich Nietzsche
Thus Spake Zaruthra

this book is dedicated to the trees

to the birds that sing

to the bees

and of course the weeds

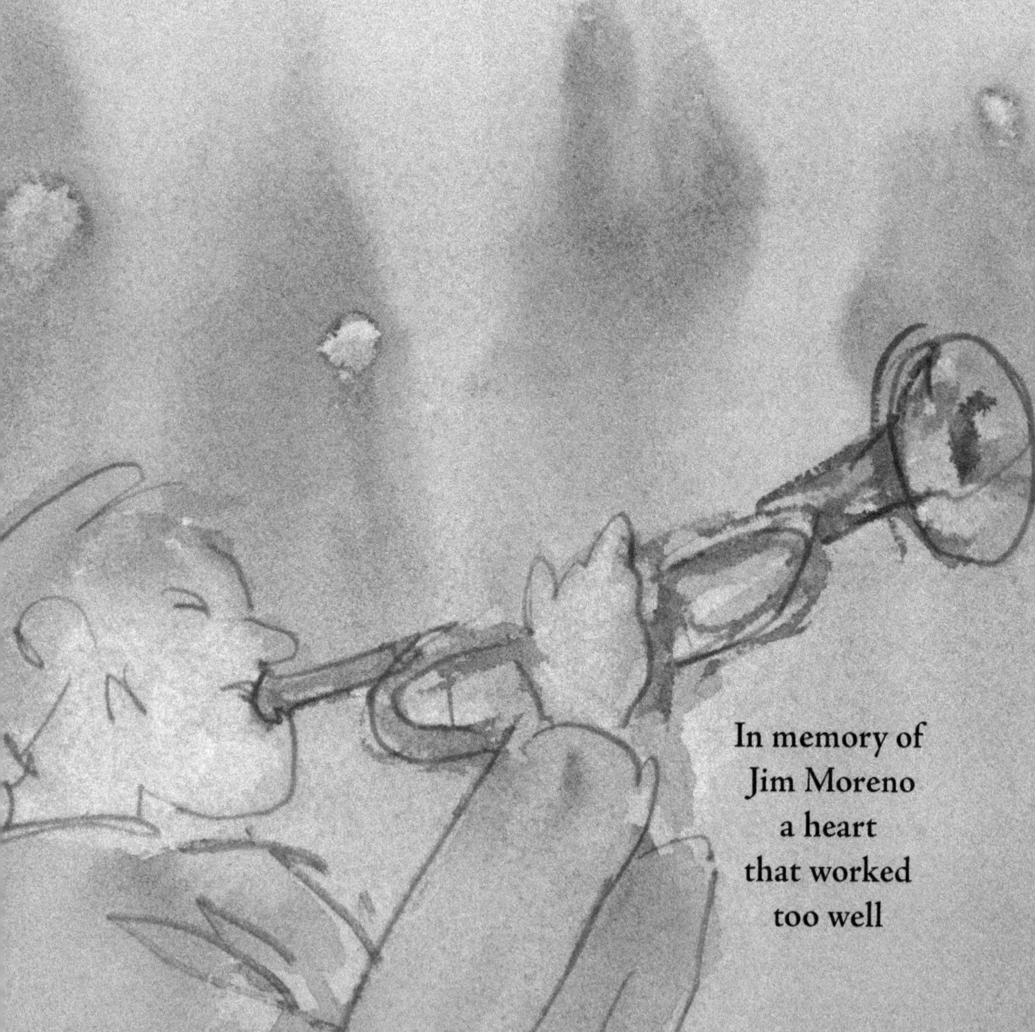

In memory of
Jim Moreno
a heart
that worked
too well

"Some people, in order to discover God,
read books. But there is a great book:
the very appearance of created things.
Look above you! Look below you!
Read it. God, whom you want to discover,
never wrote that book with ink.
Instead, He set before your eyes
the things that He had made.
Can you ask for a louder voice than that?"

–Augustine of Hippo

the Cæsura

The way I format my poems is something I found in a critique group by Curran Jeffrey, a beloved member of the San Diego poetry scene who passed away in 2023. By happenstance, one stanza in my poem had an extra gap in the middle of each line, where I paused a bit in my reading. Most wanted to correct it, only seeing it as an error. But Curran didn't see this as wrong, but as different, and creative.

That's a cæsura, pronounced "say-sura", and they used to do this in poetry all the time.

Like the Lord's prayer, where it goes…

the lord // is my shepherd
I shall // not want

The whole biblical passage is doing this. It is simply the pause in the middle of a line of verse.

When doing scansion to study the meter it's marked by double slashes. It's usually associated with middle English but can be found in ancient Hebrew, Persian and Greek poetry.

All I did was make this visible, and useful, but Curran gave it a name, and naming things is how we make the world. You wake up and see all you did before as wrong, with no idea if what you are doing is better, but your new way seems to fit instead of being a struggle. In rewriting every prior poem, I realized this was always hidden in my writing.

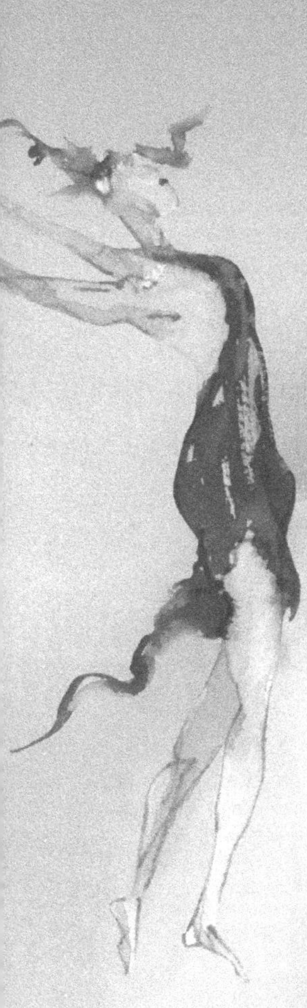

Everyone asks, how to read it; read it however you want, but it's meant to be read across, with a pause as you go, it's still a line, it's not meant to be two separate poems side by side (though often there is poetry hidden there too). In reading my poems, I might at times ignore the cæsura, other times I treat each part as if they were separate consecutive lines.

Feel free to improvise with my poems, to yourself or aloud. Read it backwards and upside down, repeat lines, skip lines, find your own poems. That is what poetry truly is, playing with words.

I use it to help me vary the pace of my reading on stage to match the music's rhythm, so I can omit these to speed things up, or treat each as if they are separate lines to slow things down. Having that space visible also for some reason makes it easier for me to read them as spoken word.

I never read a poem the same way twice, to me it's all about improvising. It allows jazz into my poetry, for each poem to breathe.

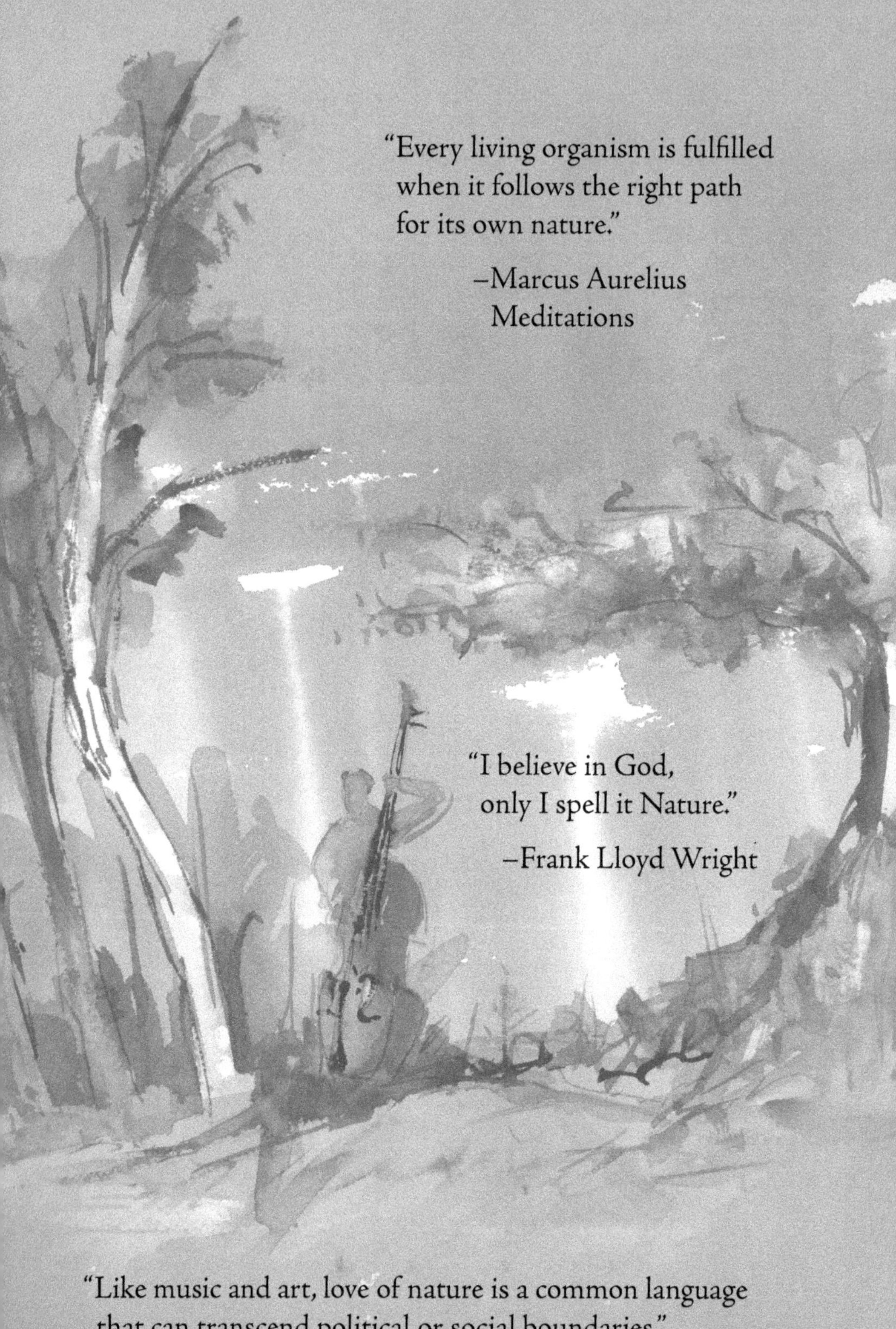

"Every living organism is fulfilled
when it follows the right path
for its own nature."
–Marcus Aurelius
Meditations

"I believe in God,
only I spell it Nature."
–Frank Lloyd Wright

"Like music and art, love of nature is a common language
that can transcend political or social boundaries."
–Jimmy Carter

out of   mythology

THE SONG OF THE FOREST

this rhyme   of history

editing note

There is no capitalism in this book, every word is lowercase, each letter fallen with the exception of I. This is the forest where nothing is proper, every letter just a weed, except the trunks of trees.

These poems do not have titles. They set no clear boundaries. Shorter poems have overgrown into each other. Longer poems have been pruned apart.

As you wander this forest—it is up to you—to find your path. To choose how you read them—and where to stop.

In school I was taught to read poems in silence, that I had to figure them out like puzzles, that each poem has a correct answer, that I would be tested. It is no wonder that poetry fails to move us—when that poetry is no longer sung.

My fellow poets all said the same thing, they said read them aloud. They asked, did it move me, did I feel? That poems are not just clever things written long ago, but words arising of my now. The premise of poetry was never in thinking, never academic, but in the rawness of feelings.

When poetry started, it was not written, but given voice as spoken word sung to music. A poem's quality is not about understanding, but about being moved. In jazz they ask—did it swing? These poems are about a song, and how we hear that song. In breathing the cadence aloud, in giving each syllable voice, the patterns you breathe, they begin to sing.

You can read these to a beat, to jazz, or whatever music that moves you, whatever you happen to play. Sing aloud this song of the forest your way, whatever works for you, or even read it silently. There is no right way to read a poem.

Only then you hear the promise of all poetry, to be what birds believe.

Contents

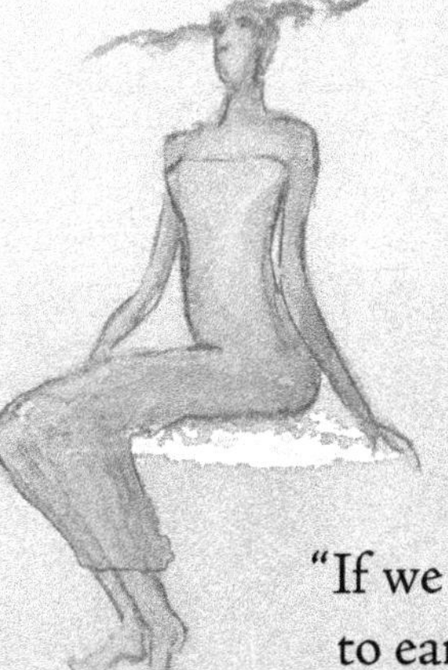

"If we surrendered
to earth's intelligence
we could rise up rooted, like trees."

–Rainer Maria Rilke

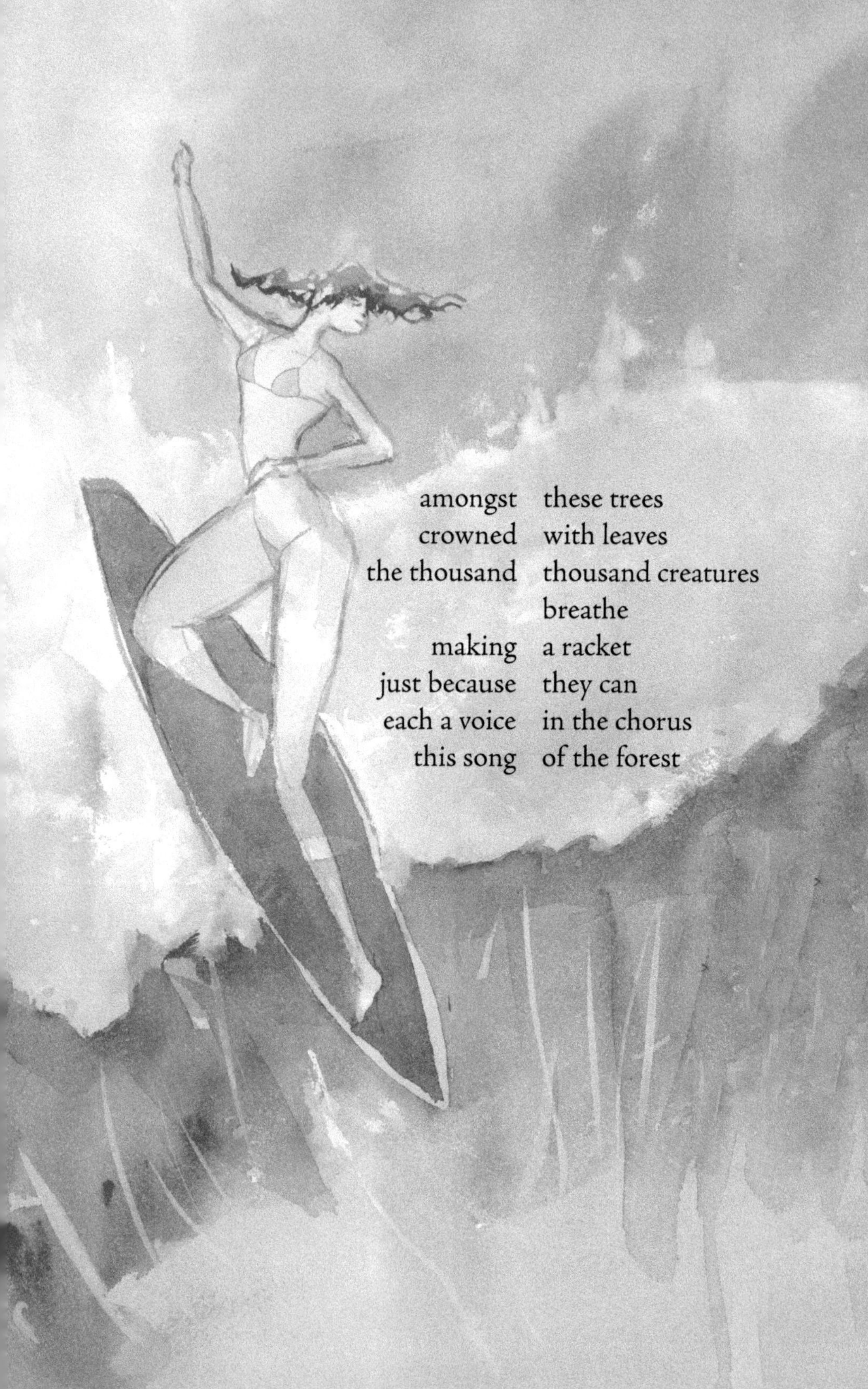
amongst   these trees
crowned   with leaves
the thousand   thousand creatures
breathe
making   a racket
just because   they can
each a voice   in the chorus
this song   of the forest

the singing
of the
leaves
the faith
of trees

the dusk reveals
fire flies
playing at being stars
crickets on their fiddles
that chorus of the lost
throwing songs into darkness
only seeing what is within
such shadows reveal my dreams

feelings be demons
when ignored
but in song
my darkness becomes
my dawn

busy birds sing
to awaken each day
voices our night
must obey

the storms of winter
where snowflakes are born

a ceremony of ice
and crystal forms
in geometric symmetry
no two the same

cold gifts of heaven
as countless as the stars
a short life measured
by falling so far
to greet the ground
the call of destiny

uniqueness then
it melts away
mingling together
into brethren below
becoming more
covering the land in snow

3

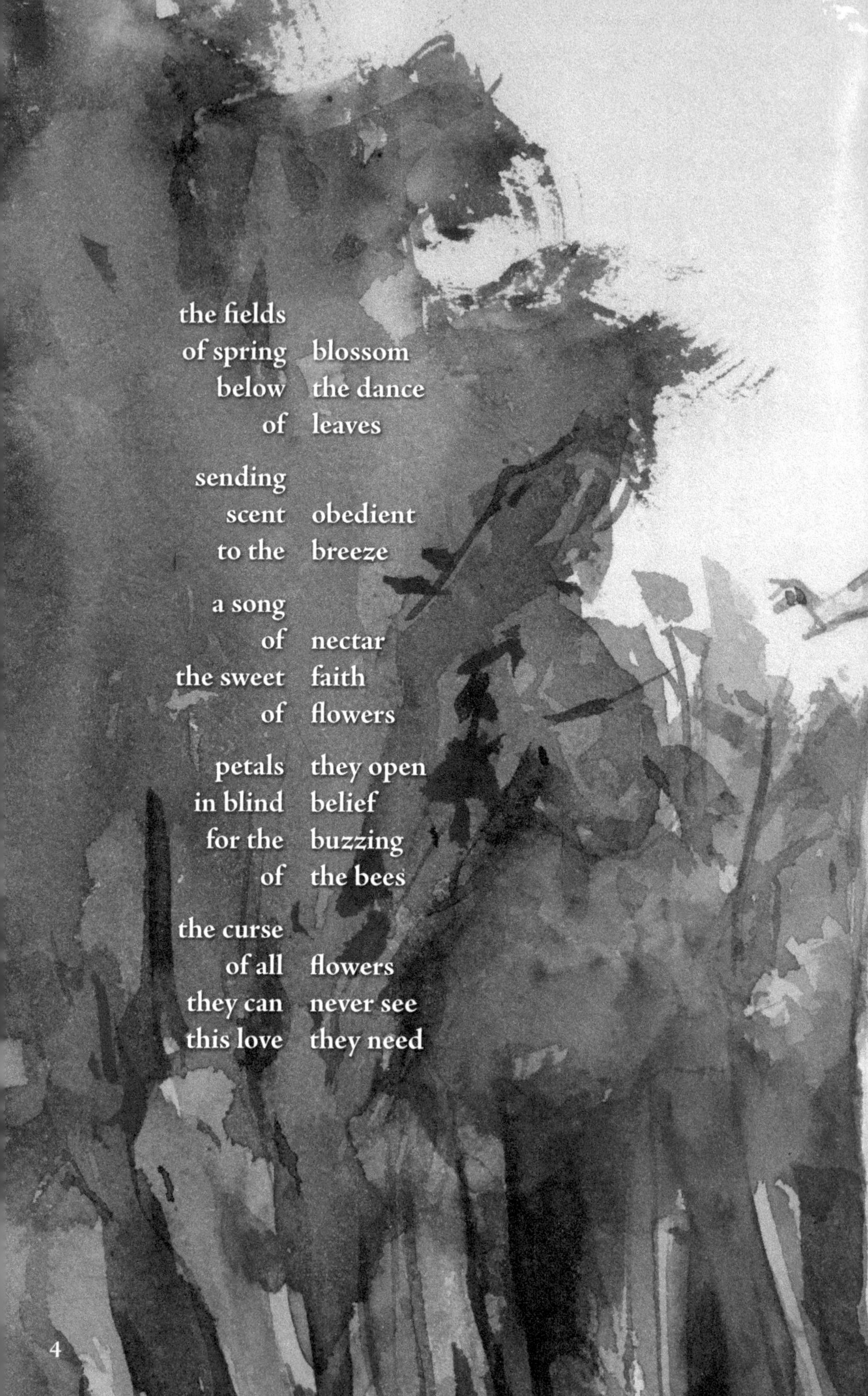

the fields
of spring   blossom
below   the dance
of   leaves

sending
scent   obedient
to the   breeze

a song
of   nectar
the sweet   faith
of   flowers

petals   they open
in blind   belief
for the   buzzing
of   the bees

the curse
of all   flowers
they can   never see
this love   they need

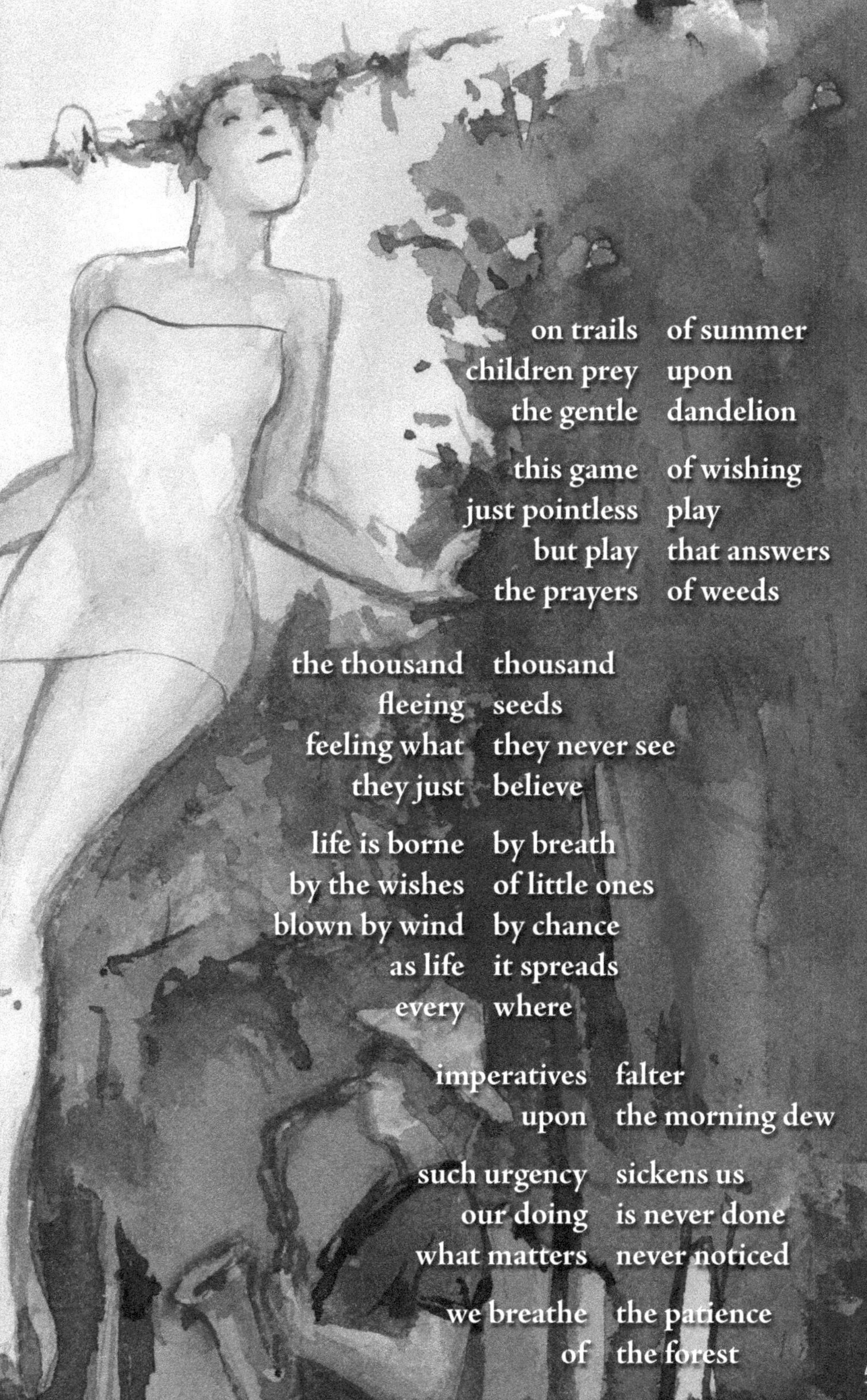

on trails   of summer
children prey   upon
the gentle   dandelion

this game   of wishing
just pointless   play
but play   that answers
the prayers   of weeds

the thousand   thousand
fleeing   seeds
feeling what   they never see
they just   believe

life is borne   by breath
by the wishes   of little ones
blown by wind   by chance
as life   it spreads
every   where

imperatives   falter
upon   the morning dew

such urgency   sickens us
our doing   is never done
what matters   never noticed

we breathe   the patience
of   the forest

the falling   leaves
have   a destiny
fading   into colors
no one   sees

upon this   forest floor
a rotting   blanket
over   the teeth
               of worms

feeding   this earth
all that   exists below
insulating   the living soil
from   the coming snow

the shivering trees
surrounded   by
surrendered   leaves
now   silent
in the   breeze

the forest   within
its   stillness
sings   in ways
we don't   believe

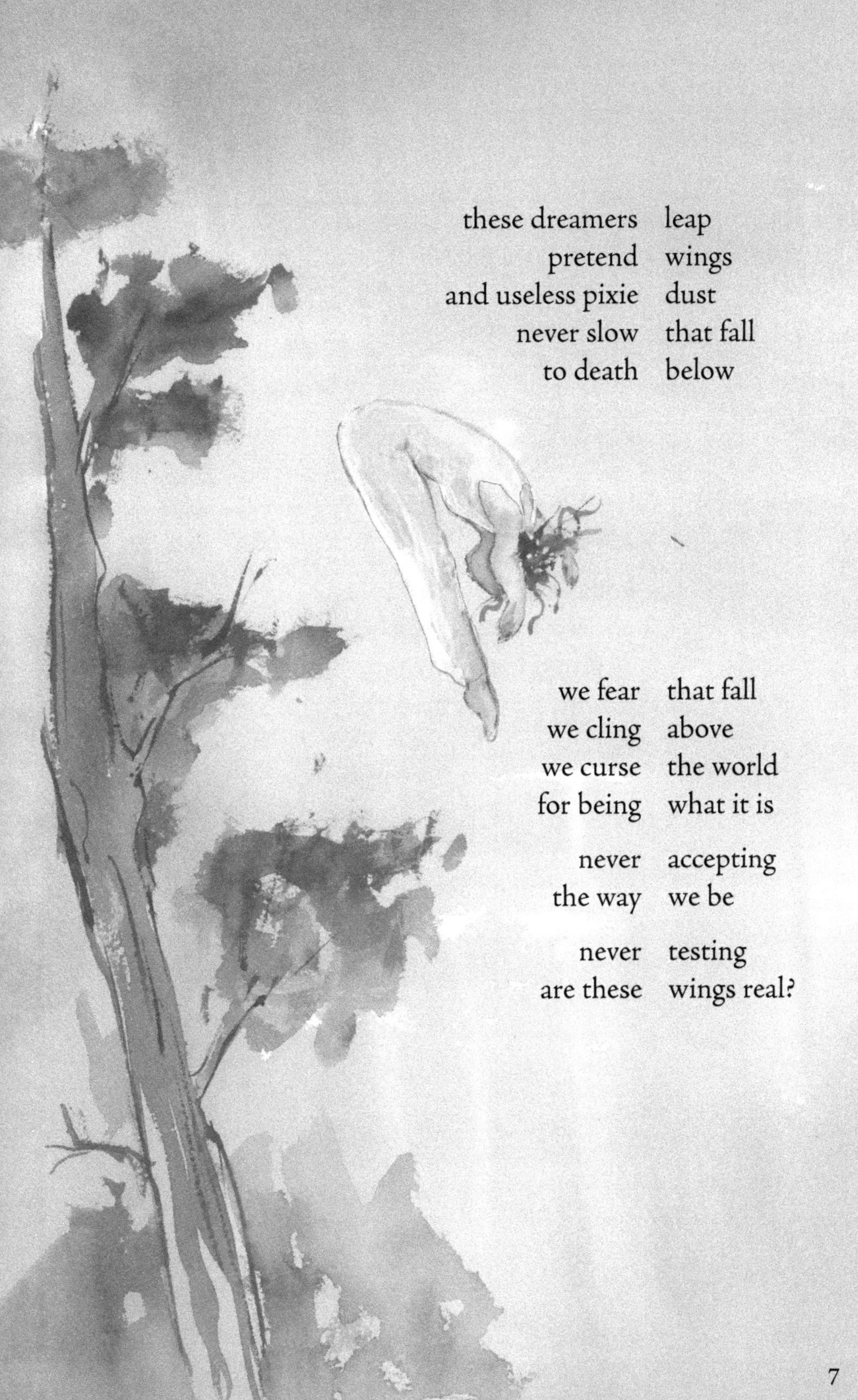

these dreamers   leap
pretend   wings
and useless pixie   dust
never slow   that fall
to death   below

we fear   that fall
we cling   above
we curse   the world
for being   what it is

never   accepting
the way   we be

never   testing
are these   wings real?

numb
we drink   to forget

in dreamless   sleep
amidst   the night
the river   lethe
consumes   our light

in mourning   of meaning
without   childish play
grounded   in reality
our work   buries the day

despite this   dream's demise
jealous of   these
foolish   few

still reaching   for
their   stars

we   laugh
we   ridicule

they   throw
their lives   away

but every   so often
a dreamer   survives
that leap   of faith

they fail   to die
they hurtle   past pain

the fallen   feel
that dream   awaken
becoming   real

the earth   I fear
that tomb   becomes
not our end   but mother
the earth   my womb

buried beneath   the light
the dream   awakens
slaying   mythology
breaking   taboos
ending   rules

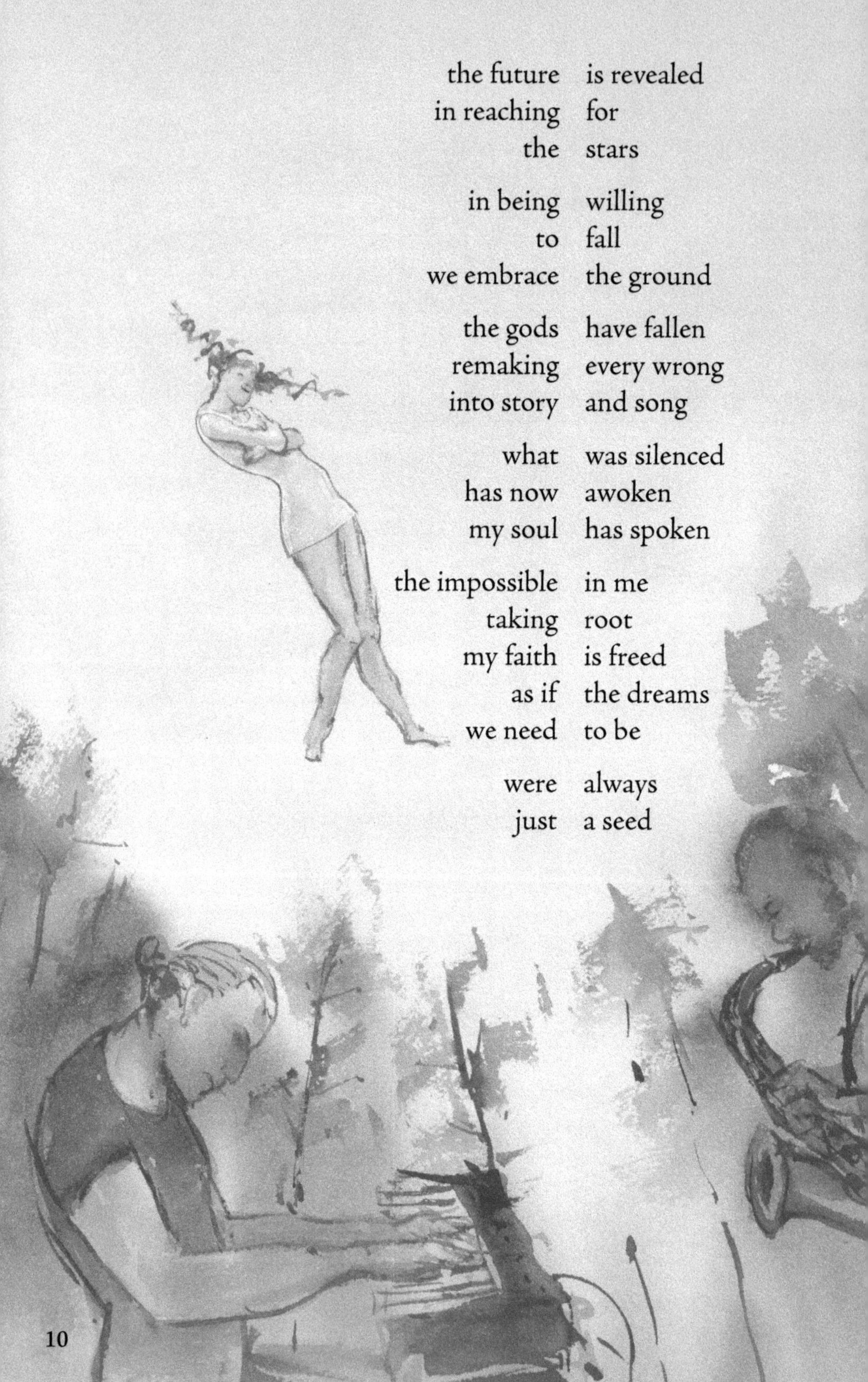

the future   is revealed
in reaching   for
the   stars

in being   willing
to   fall
we embrace   the ground

the gods   have fallen
remaking   every wrong
into story   and song

what   was silenced
has now   awoken
my soul   has spoken

the impossible in me
taking   root
my faith   is freed
as if   the dreams
we need   to be

were   always
just   a seed

for each acorn   to be born
what it was   must die

its shell   this armor
that traps   the green within
this hardness   is its coffin

to sprout   it must break
itself   out

to break
the ground   above
it must   fight
against   its nature

to see
it is   not
just   a seed

sleeping seeds   do not dream
but   ripen
into what   they are
into what   they were
meant   to be

the acorn   does not
it cannot   be taught
from voices   deep
within   its being
comes   knowing

on every   bit of it
is written   that I
I am   an oak tree

that it is   and always was
the very   instrument
upon   which
life itself   does sing

to rise to rule
this canopy of leaves
each oak tree
must grow into themselves

a justice found
in obedience
to the song

the voice of seasons
which give it cause
to sprout its leaves
upon the spring
and to drop them
upon the fall

never in decisions
but in rhythms
the cycle is all

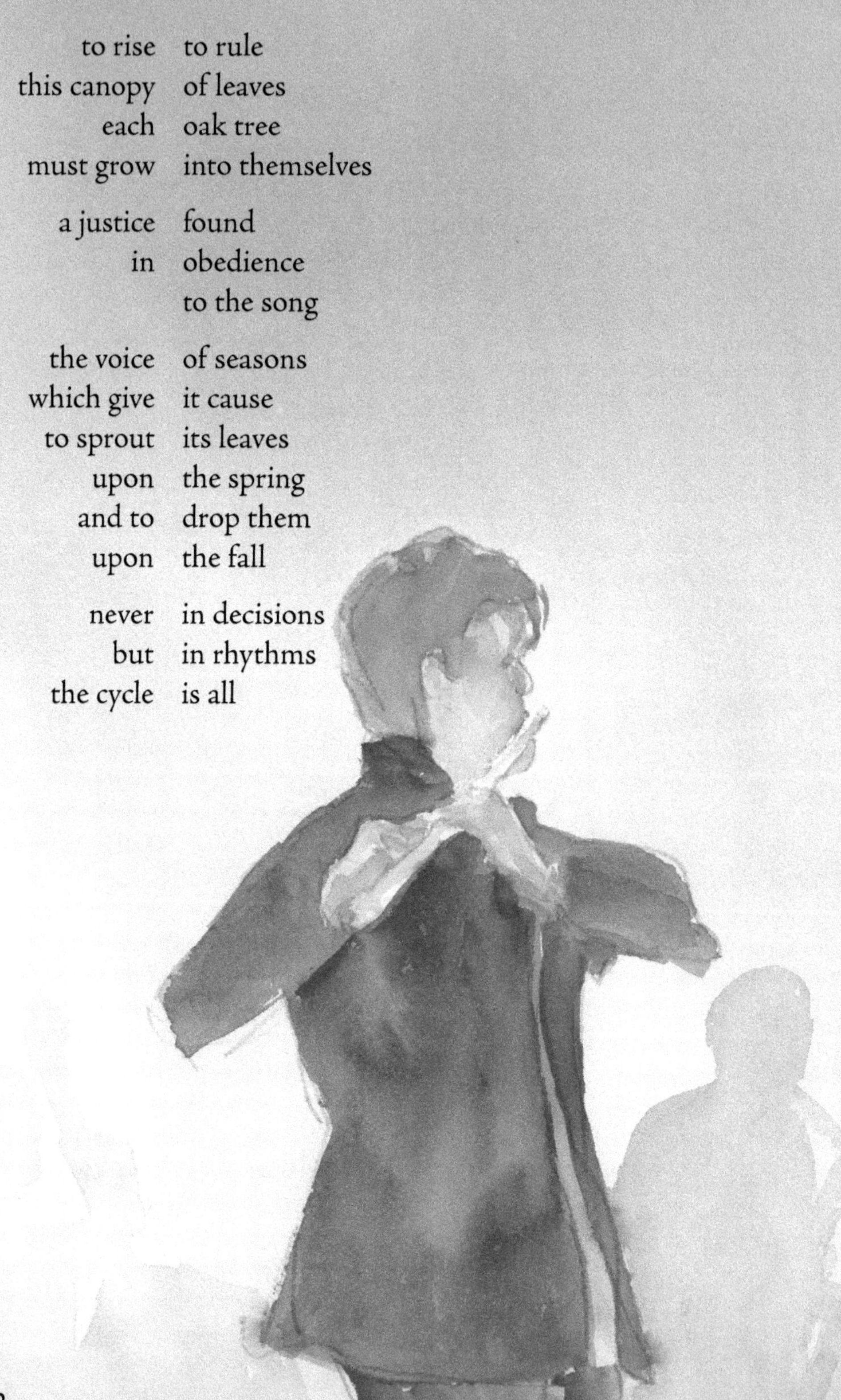

we carve
          our   initials
          upon   its bark

          we leave   our letters
          and hew   a heart

          the scar   remains
        we touched   this tree
      we disfigured   its skin

          long after
          our love   has
          moved   along

          long after
          our lives   have
          faded   away

        what others   have carved
                      into us

        the wounds
           remain   within
        this debris   of memory

          the trees   above
              they   remember
        our knives   of love

this solitary tree
dared grow
where no tree
belongs

its seed had fallen
into this granite crack
a crevice that defined
its destiny

clinging here
upon bare cliff walls
looking down upon
the forest far below
with gentle earth denied
the root bound
cannot thrive

persistence
is not innate
but driven
it is learned
within the struggle

what I endure
is what I must
survive

clarity is found
in this wrestling
against the solidity
of stone

the forest   feels
the pride   of trees
in this   solitary
rise   above

the crowd   can never feel
the struggle   of your heart
that effort   over years
each   meeting
with   failure
and   fear

these roots   I own
what   no other
can feel   or know
the substance   of my story
is mine   alone

in denial   of my doubt
I just   did it
day   by day
the pain   the sacrifice

the forest   only sees
another   fallen seed
that   dared grow
where   no tree
dared grow   before

we never   see
how we   are known
when we   rise
and fall   alone

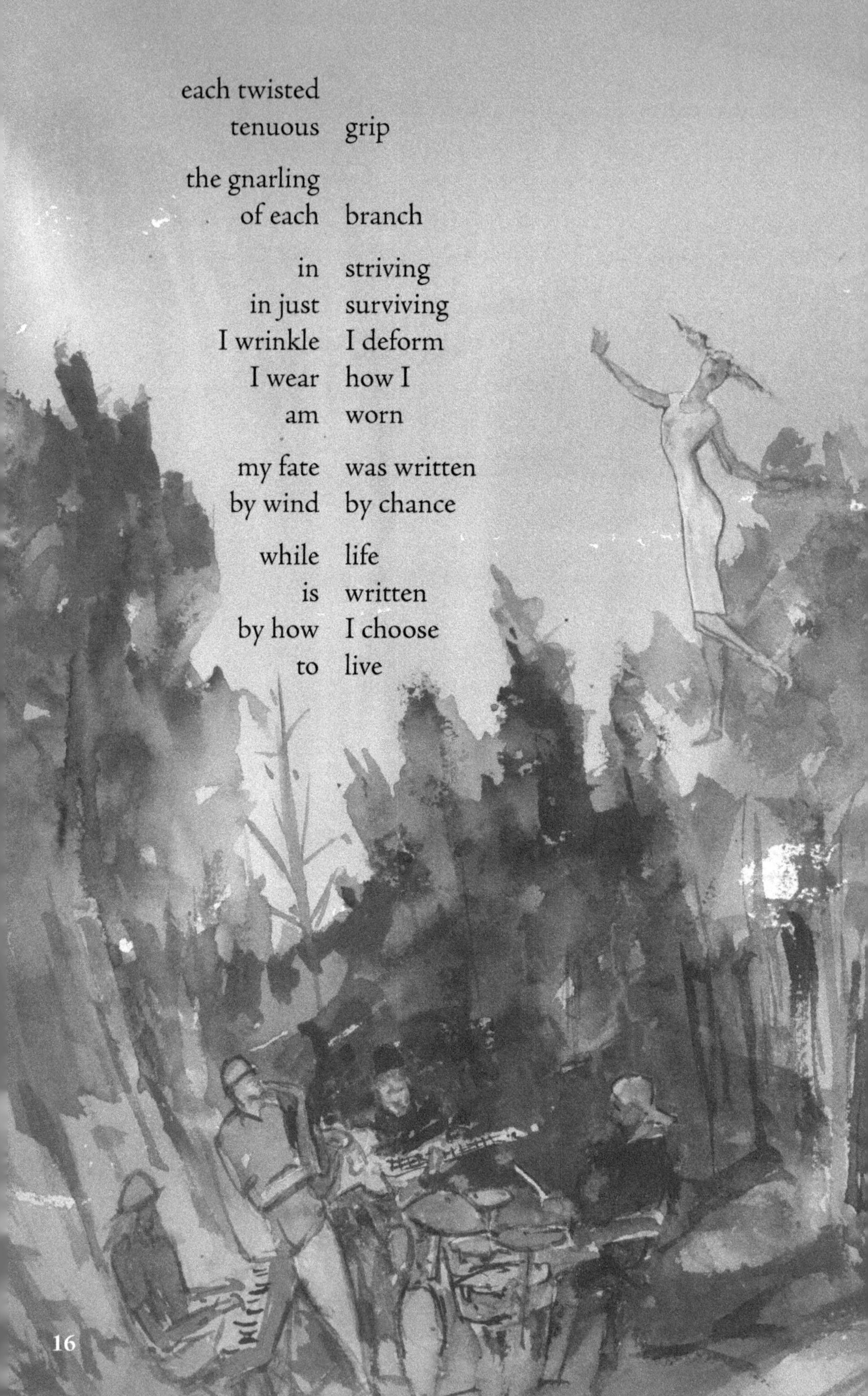

each twisted
tenuous   grip

the gnarling
of each   branch

in   striving
in just   surviving
I wrinkle   I deform
I wear   how I
am   worn

my fate   was written
by wind   by chance

while   life
is   written
by how   I choose
to   live

the grass   knows
no   other side

there is   no greener
life is   either

more   green
or more   brown

grass   cannot move
grass   cannot choose
it just grows   the best it can

just as the weeds   do not choose
where   they fall

the virtue   of weeds
we hold them   guilty for this

is in   growing
anywhere

and   everywhere

despite   it all

ground   is ground
a broken home   is a home

the forest   moves
in its   own way
at its   own speed

what matters   time?

to a presence   in each
moment

to a patience   outlasting
history

what is   eternity
to a   tree?

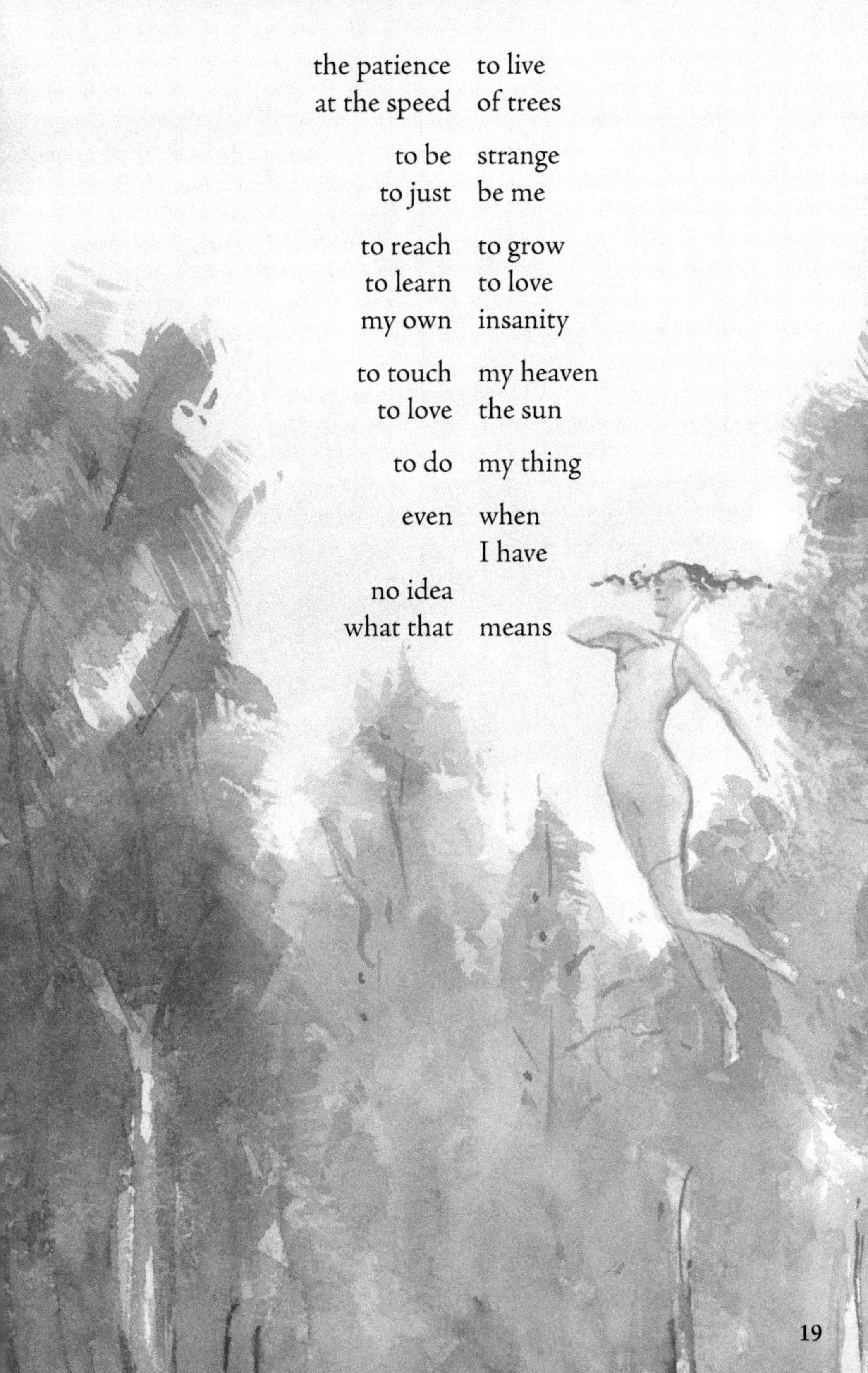

the patience to live
at the speed of trees

to be strange
to just be me

to reach to grow
to learn to love
my own insanity

to touch my heaven
to love the sun

to do my thing

even when
I have
no idea
what that means

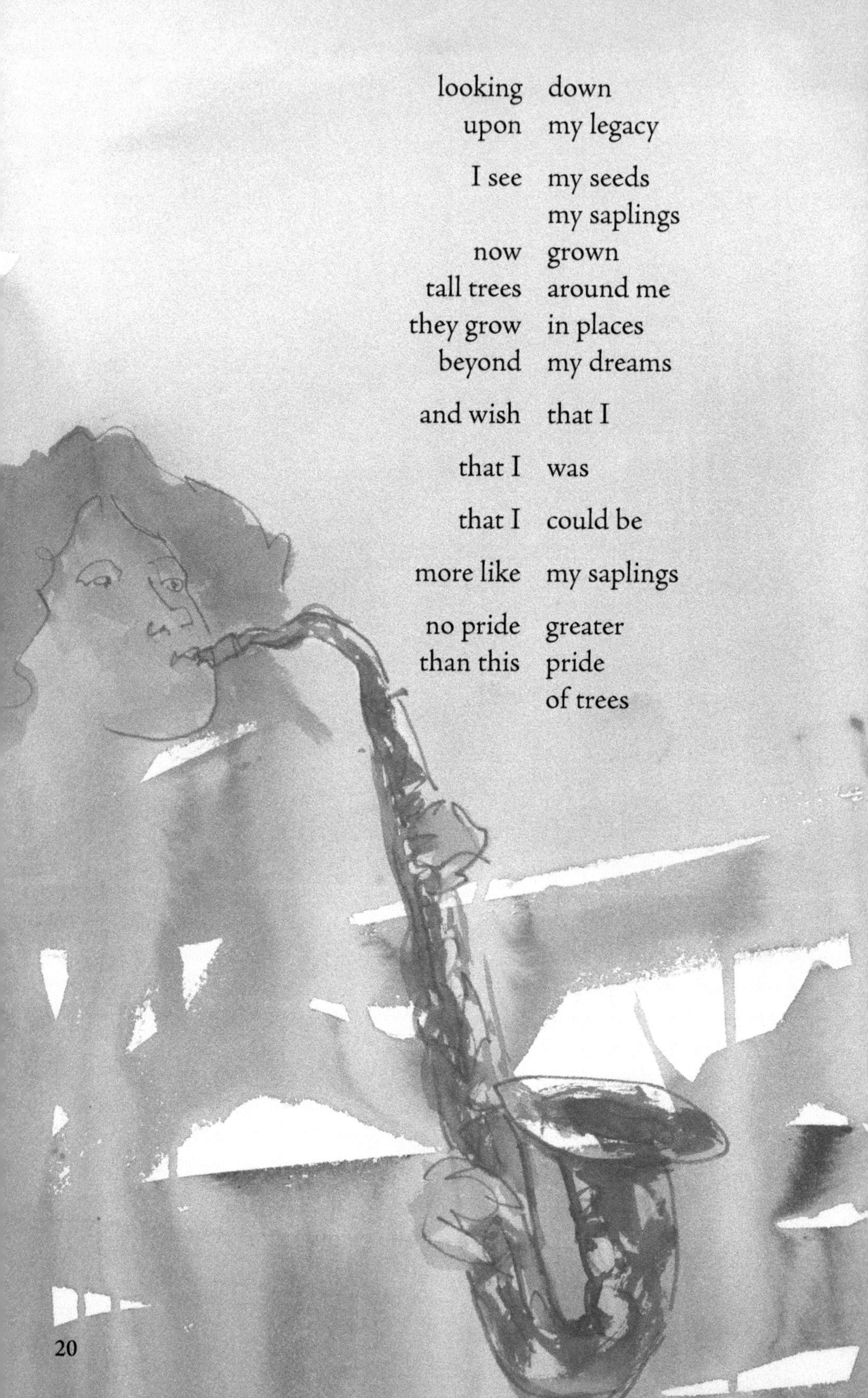

looking   down
upon   my legacy

I see   my seeds
my saplings
now   grown
tall trees   around me
they grow   in places
beyond   my dreams

and wish   that I

that I   was

that I   could be

more like   my saplings

no pride   greater
than this   pride
of trees

there is no song
without an end

nothing sings forever
centuries pass
it fades and grays
lowering its gaze

no longer reaching
for the sun

falling down to crash upon
this fragile earth

each fallen log
a sacrifice upon
this forest floor

our elders fall
to each passing year
to that tyrant time
the truth that rules
this span of lives

the kiss of kronos
that titan of time
consumes us all
consumes all gods

no king nor general
commands this
bite of years

our time has passed
making this
the sapling's time
to rise

these rings   of age
carved   by seasons
in joy   and trauma
our self   each year
  revealing

in each   wrinkle
of   its reaching
with scars   of love
  inscribed

this voice
revealed   in life
has   become
the elegy

  in dying

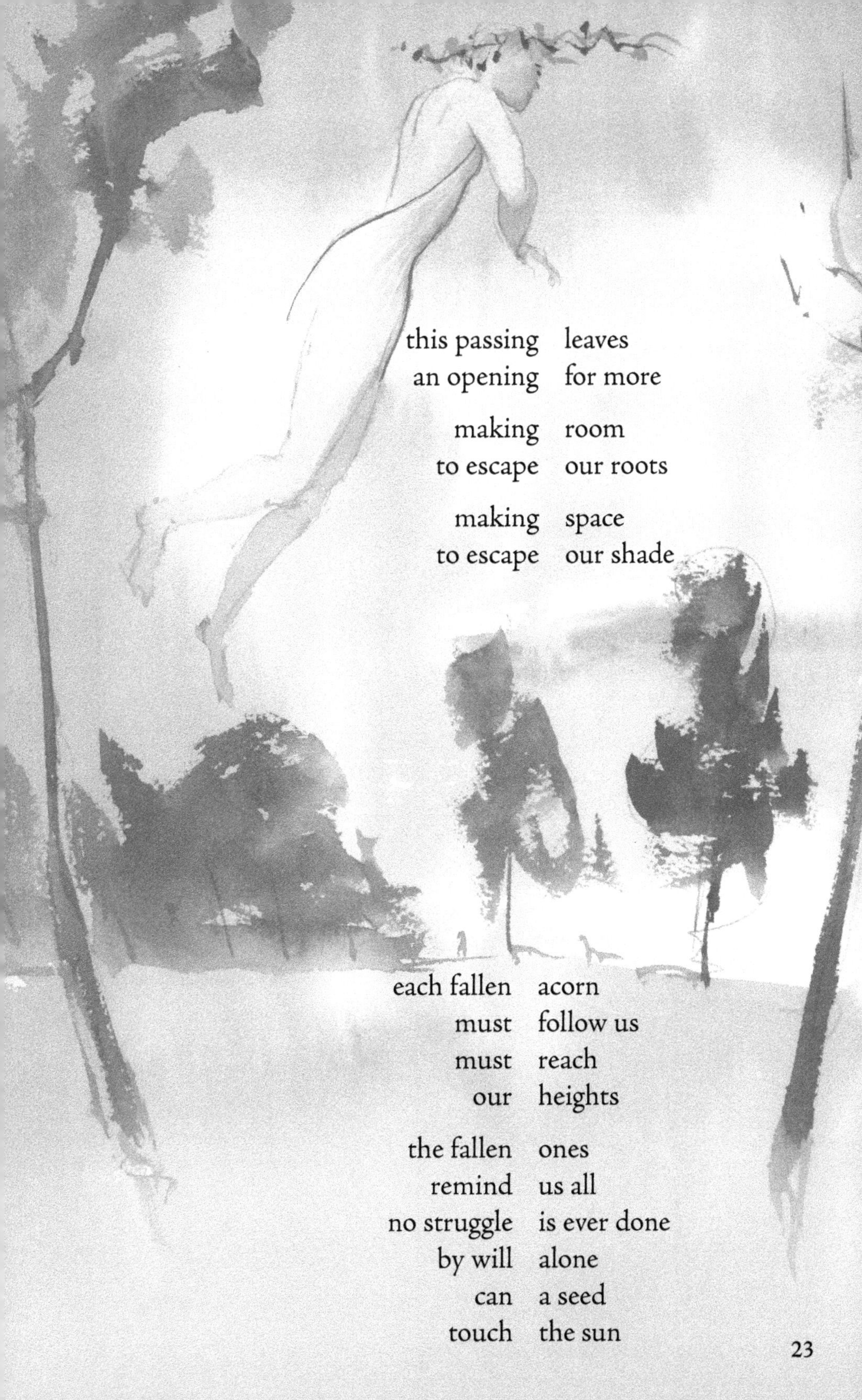

this passing   leaves
an opening   for more

making   room
to escape   our roots

making   space
to escape   our shade

each fallen   acorn
must   follow us
must   reach
our   heights

the fallen   ones
remind   us all
no struggle   is ever done
by will   alone
can   a seed
touch   the sun

23

we lost   a tree
and   no one heard

did   it happen?

did it   make a sound?

to live   in such silence
with no one   to hear

no one   to attend
never   a funeral

no one   is aware
no obituary   nor grave

no one   to mourn
no marker   or name
no one   to care

a loneliness   so great
you cease   to exist
you never   existed

has   a tree
ever   heard?

ever   seen
or   tasted?

ever   sensed
the   senses
of smell
and   touch?

lacking   these
          five senses
what we   believe
how we   define
all living   things

a tree   must be
a senseless   unthinking
            unfeeling
            thing

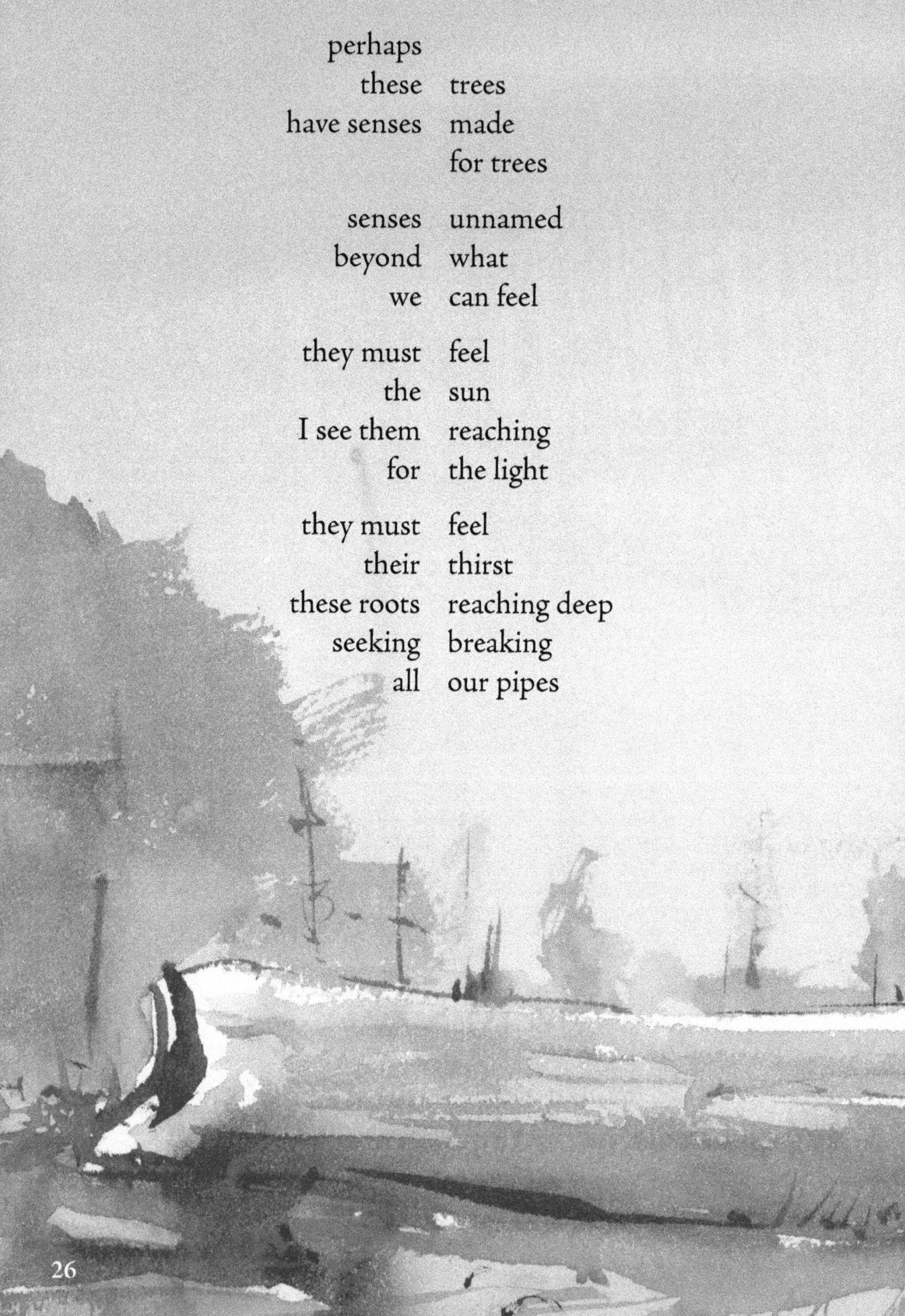

perhaps
  these   trees
have senses made
           for trees

  senses unnamed
  beyond what
     we can feel

they must feel
    the sun
I see them reaching
    for the light

they must feel
  their thirst
these roots reaching deep
  seeking breaking
    all our pipes

they must   feel
the roots   of
each   neighbor

in depth   connecting
roots reaching   touching
perhaps   even hugging

they must   feel
entangled   in community
an underground
unspoken   society

they must   feel
their   pain
and sing   and dream
in ways   that I
cannot   imagine

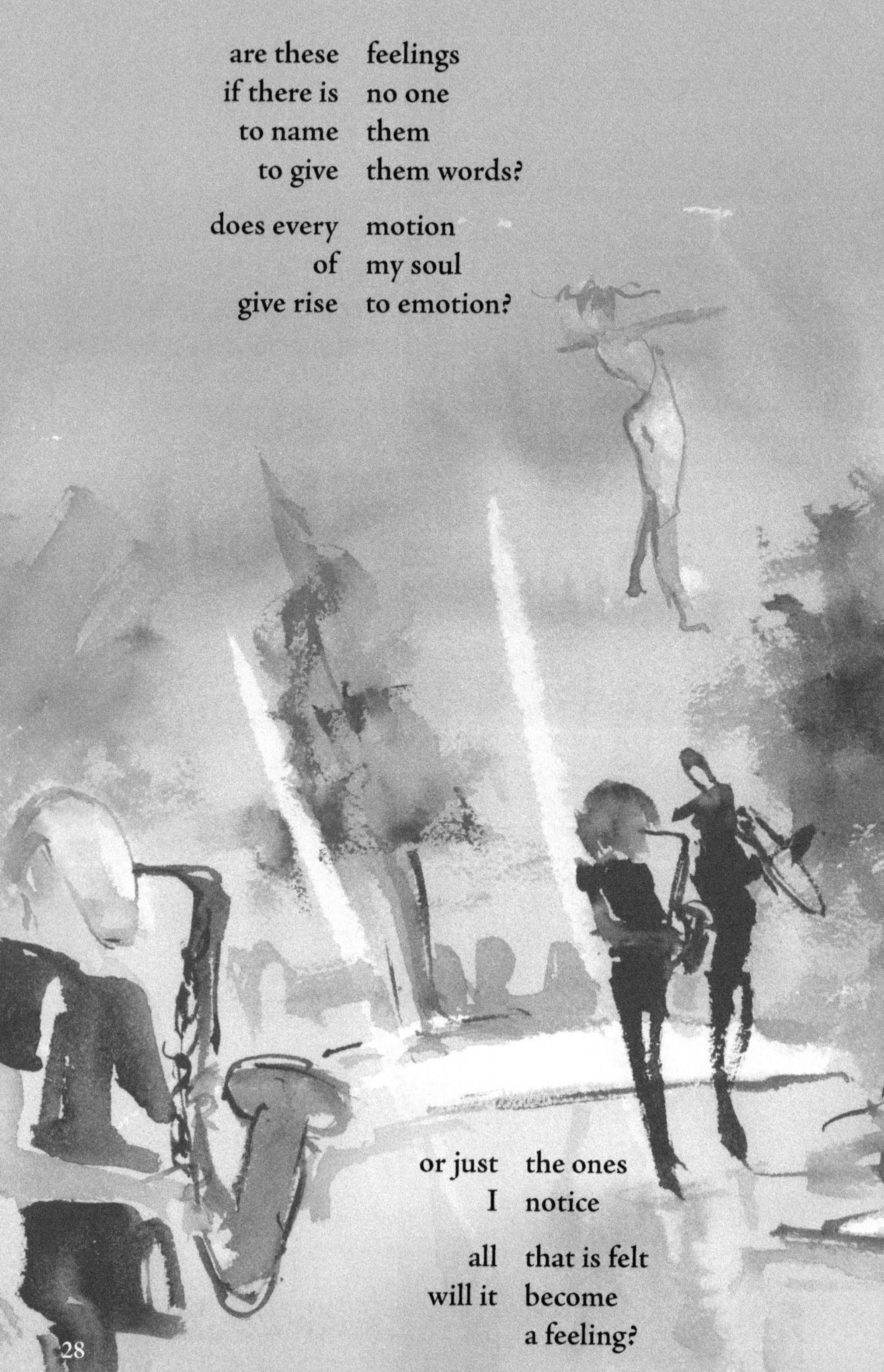

are these   feelings
if there is   no one
to name   them
to give   them words?

does every motion
of   my soul
give rise   to emotion?

or just   the ones
I   notice

all   that is felt
will it   become
            a feeling?

28

to make   it conscious
to make   it known
does a feeling   have to be
    perceived?

when unwritten   unsaid
when   there is
no record   or memory

did   I feel?

is a poem   still a poem
with no one   to read it?

when no one   has heard it?

when those   around us
refuse   to listen?

can   a feeling
I feel   alone
be   real?

we lose   ourselves
in   the struggle

to win   you need
a loser
for every   eater
there is   the eaten

that all   existence
is a   competition
the survival of   the fittest
is   now
competing   with religion

darwin   in his descent
suggested
that singing   came
before   speaking

the melody
that must   be heard
that   cannot be
put into   words

...

is   unheard

we lose   ourselves
in   the struggle

we forget   to sing

never   the possible

never   to belong

never that   nature

evolved   to
the   song

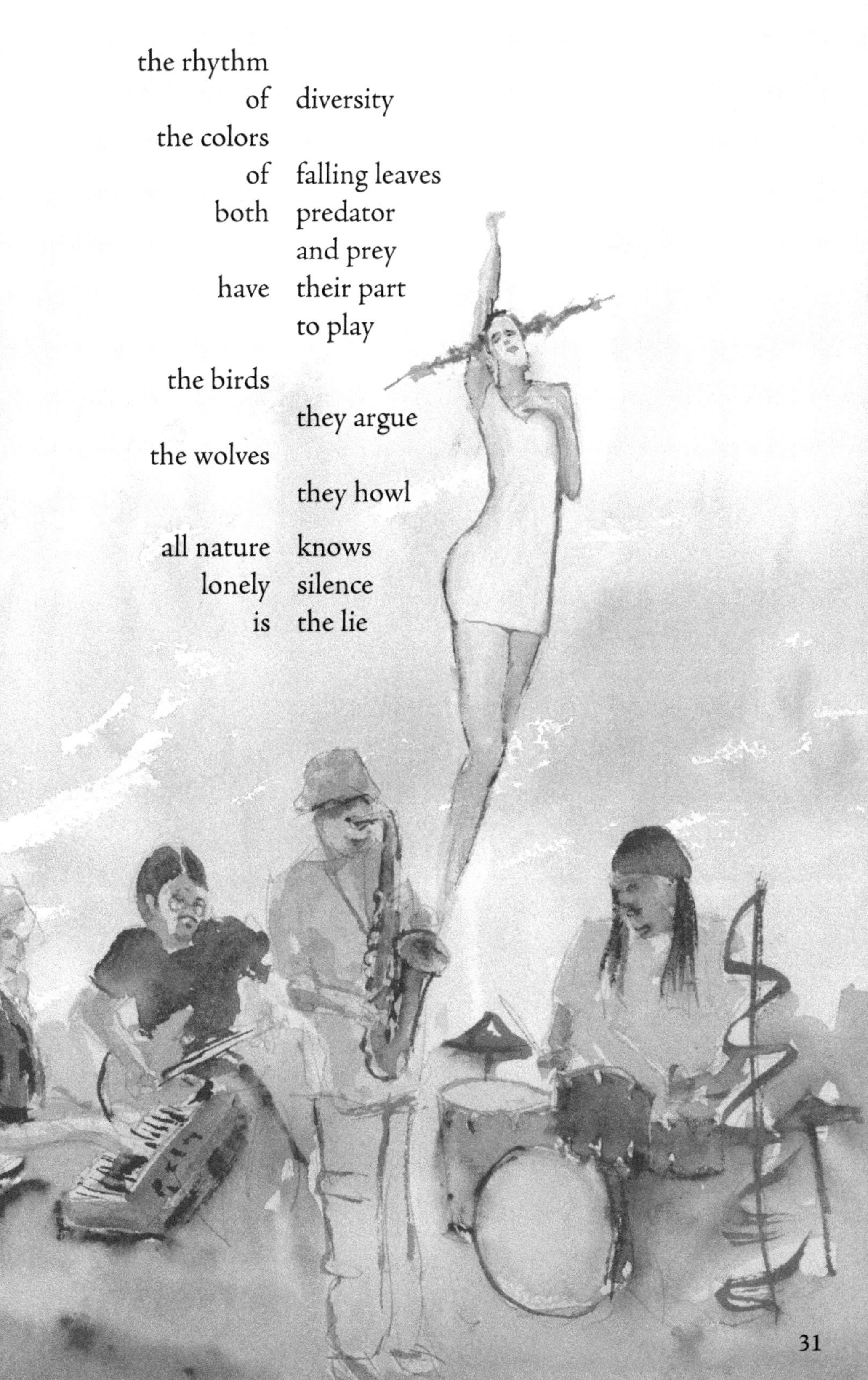

the rhythm
of   diversity
the colors
of   falling leaves
both   predator
and prey
have   their part
to play

the birds
they argue
the wolves
they howl

all nature   knows
lonely   silence
is   the lie

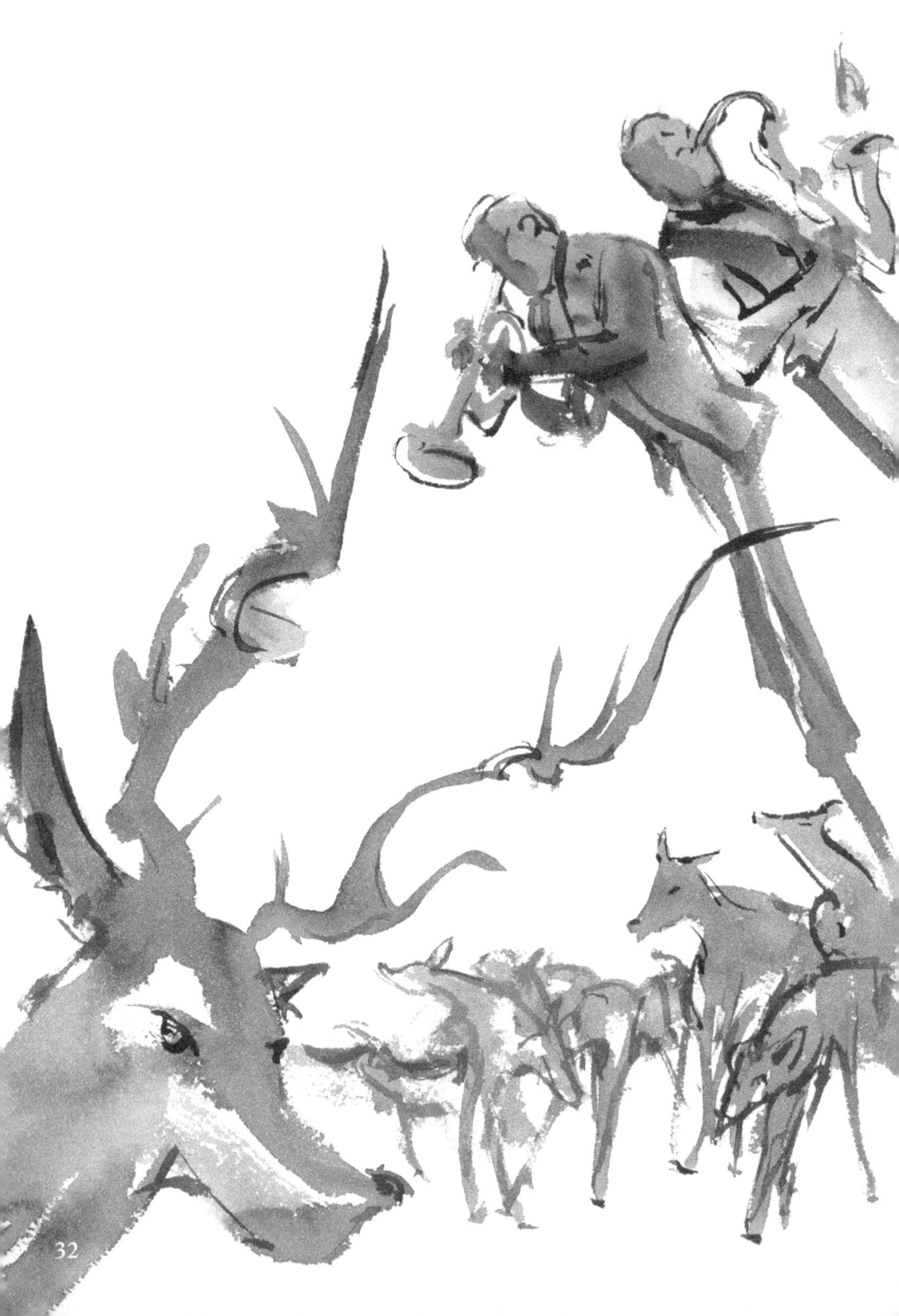

just   listen
  in   your stillness

close

        your eyes
exhale

        exhale more

then   hold it

hear

        that
pause

        within

just   listen
  to   your heart
to all that
 you   ignore

the truth   is hidden
beneath   your beating
behind   your breathing

your beating   heart
the heart   of every
living   thing

each heart   it beats
upon   a metronome
of being

nature   it sings
in each   and every
single thing

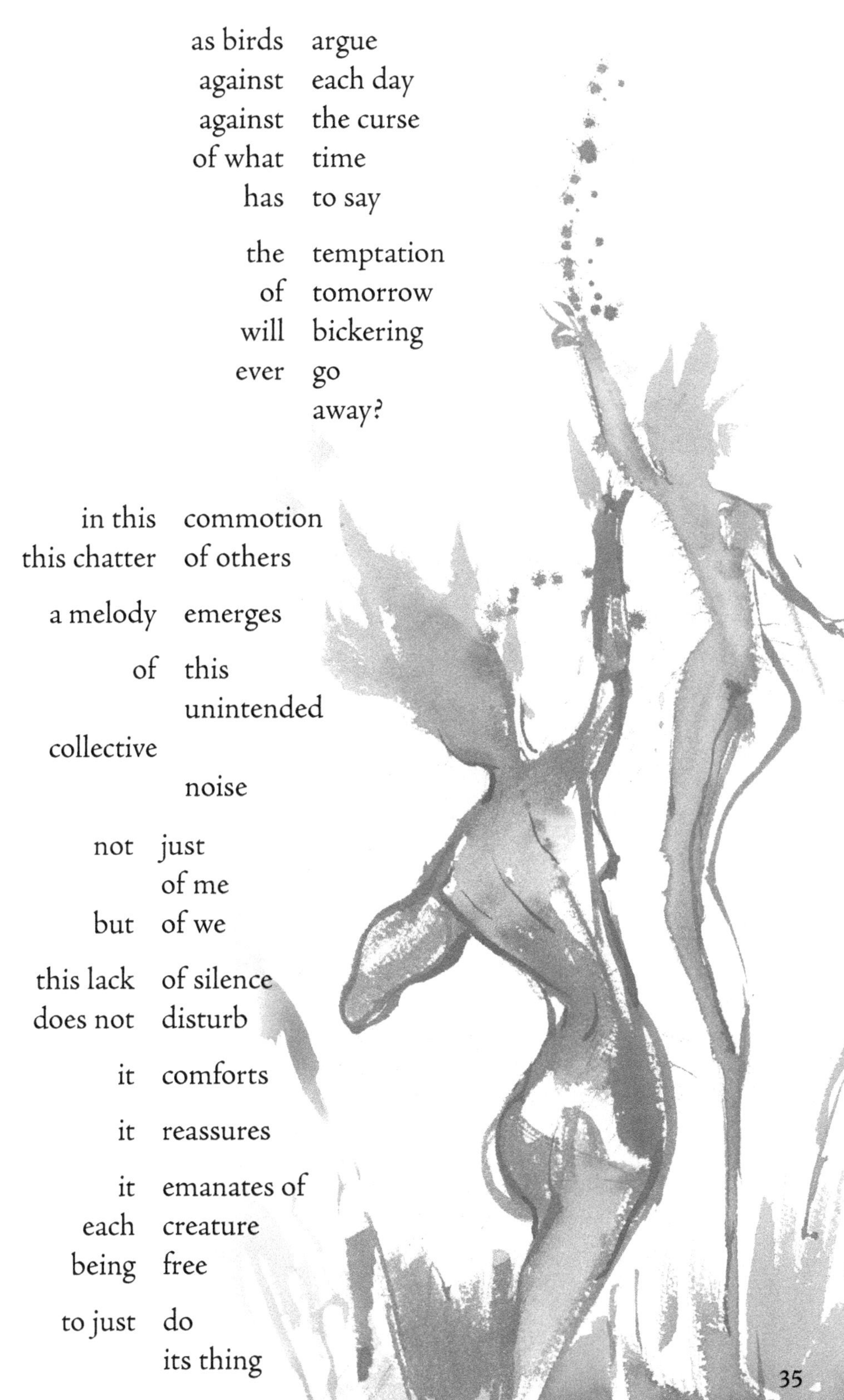

as birds argue
against each day
against the curse
of what time
has to say

the temptation
of tomorrow
will bickering
ever go
away?

in this commotion
this chatter of others

a melody emerges

of this
unintended

collective

noise

not just
of me

but of we

this lack of silence
does not disturb

it comforts

it reassures

it emanates of
each creature
being free

to just do
its thing

the song
is in   being alive
the   vibration
felt
upon   our lives
we   flock together
or we   fly alone
in each   decision
in just   doing
our   thing
we   become
unintended   instruments
upon   which
creation   sings

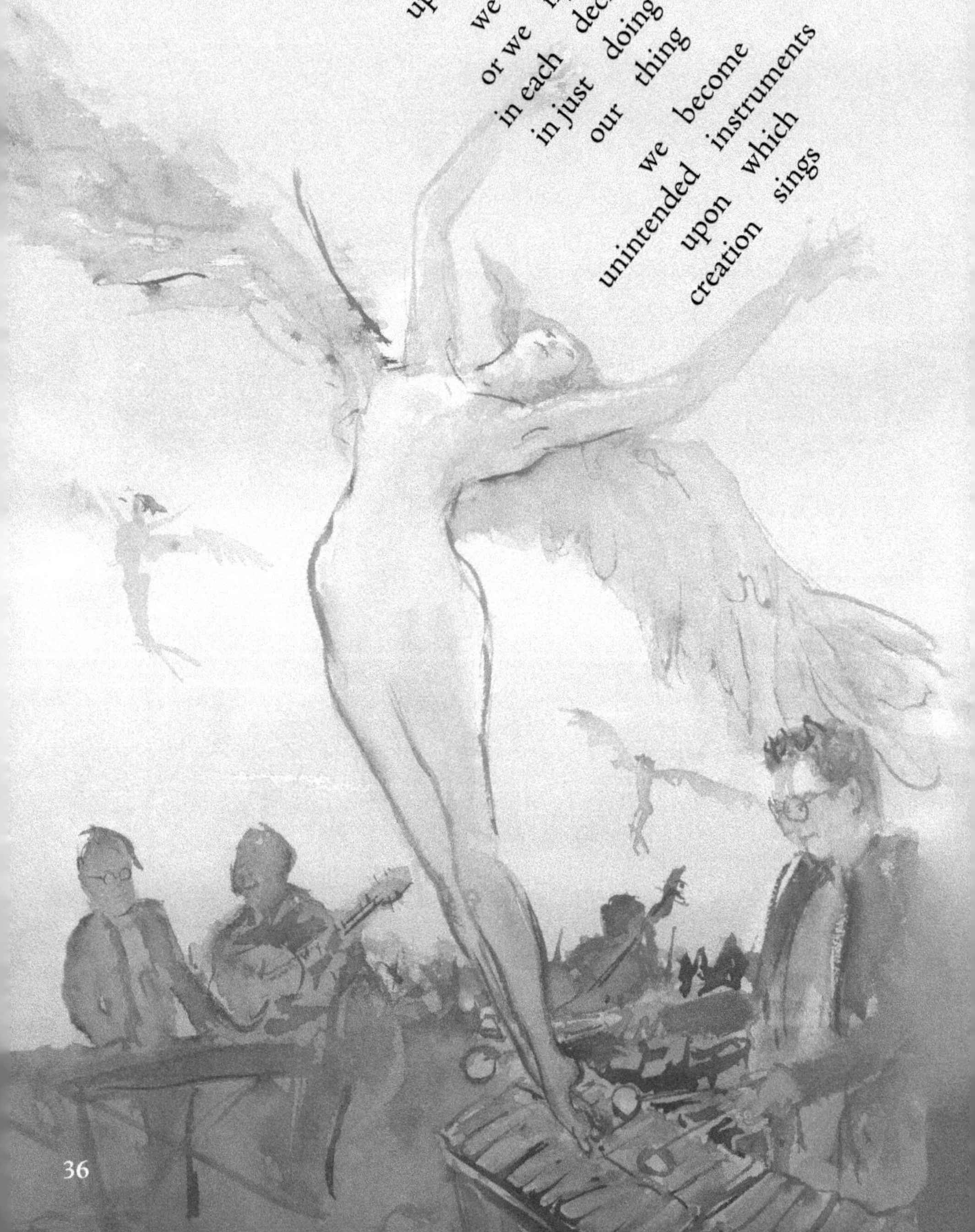

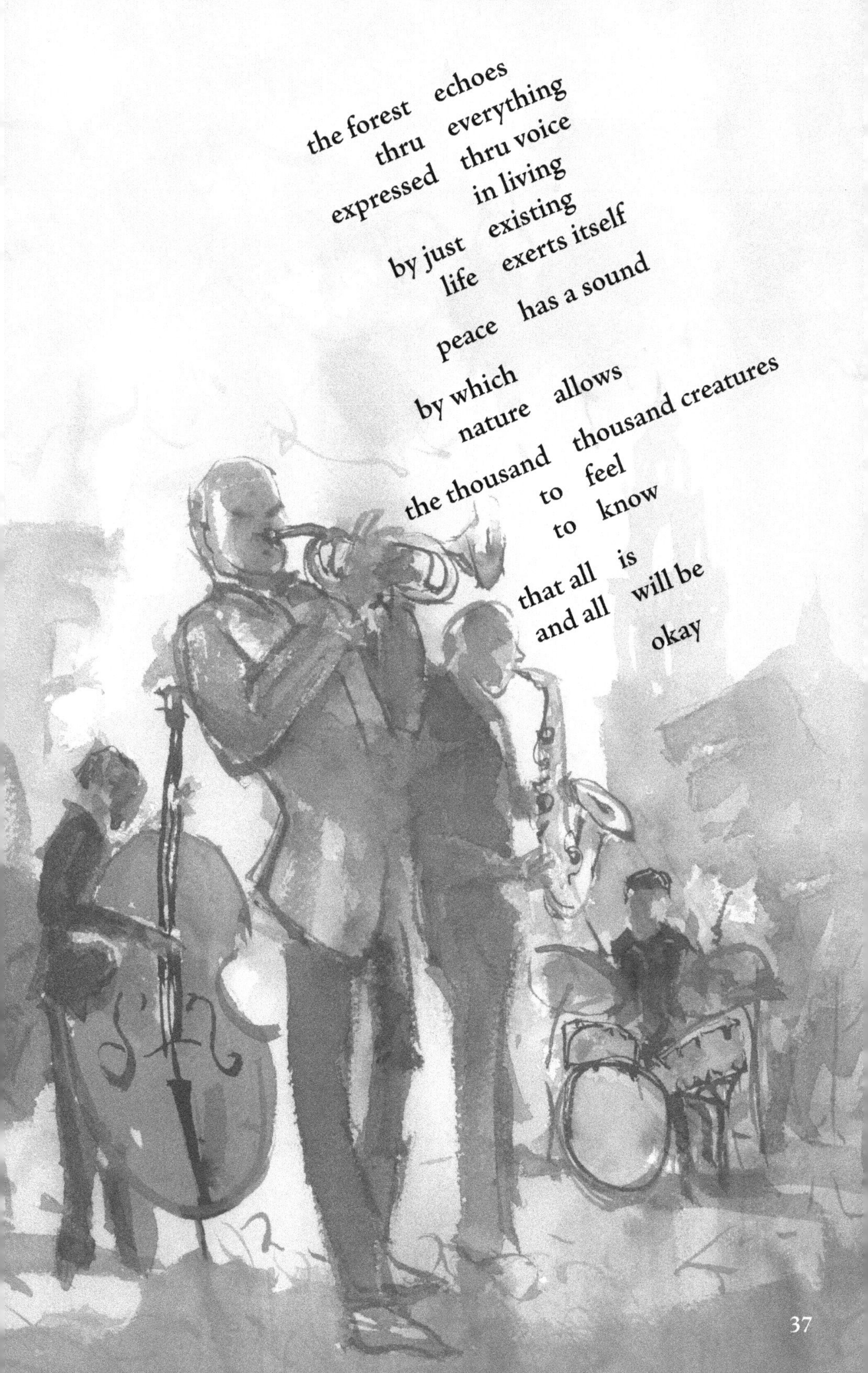

the forest   echoes
    thru   everything
expressed   thru voice
       in living
by just   existing
life   exerts itself
peace   has a sound

by which
nature   allows
the thousand   thousand creatures
       to   feel
       to   know
that all   is
and all   will be
       okay

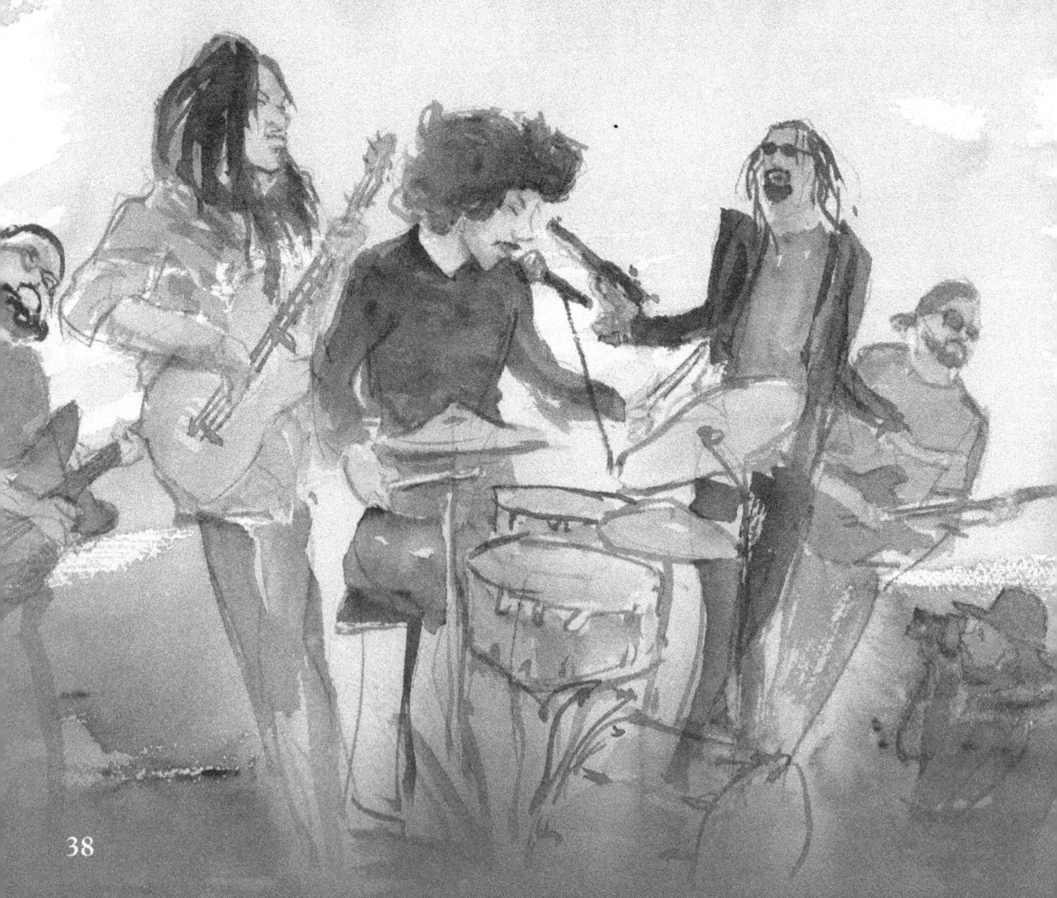

<pre>
never   to hear
           the angels
their song of love

      nor   the demons
       of   their fall

that unheard scream
      thru   eternity

   within   this silence
  we call   hell
</pre>

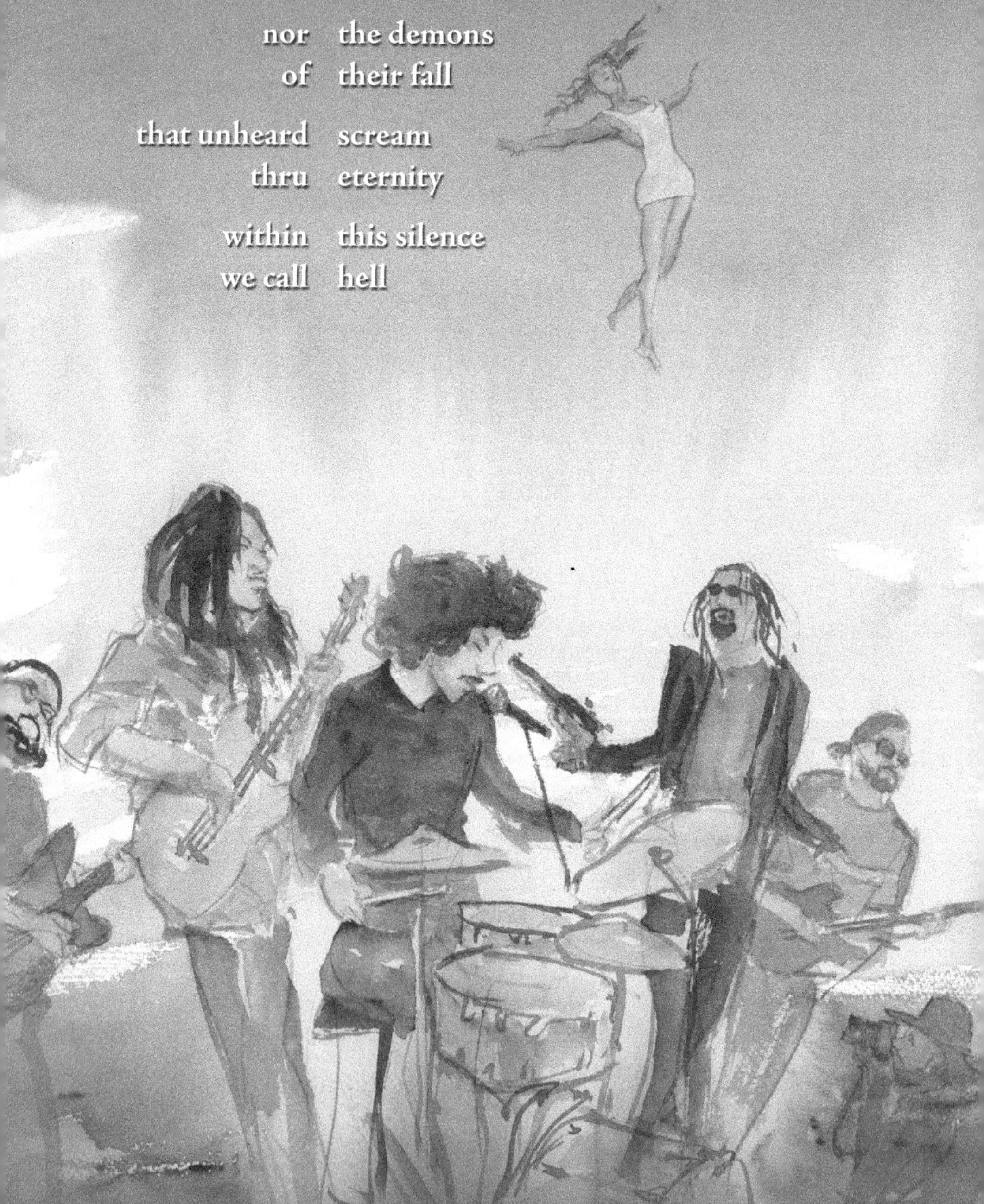

the hymn
in myth

we sing to
gods forgotten

what   was humanity?
before   words
before   language
before   that tower?
when babel   fell?

what   were we?
before   god's curse?
before language   divided us?
did we   sing together?
before speaking   apart?

it is by words   our mind does breathe
that   we realize
   we be
and yet   I fear …
unspoken   seas

hidden urges   dwell
unnamed desires   dream
voiceless longings   drown
unheard   demons
rule this   darkness
beneath my   being

can I   even feel?
when it fails   to fit
   into words?

we feel   this primal song
my un-worded   it rages to be
to be   set free

is this   madness?
are these demons   me?

without   the light
of words   to carry them
our thoughts   suffocate
screaming   to be freed
it is then   I howl
it is then   I sing

we got it   wrong
we forgot   the song
words are   but echoes
of our   thinking

long   before words
we lived   in myth
we prayed   we dreamed
we sang   we loved

listen close   my love
in the   silence
between   us
we speak   in spaces
we wander   impossible paths
we write   our song
   yet unheard
beyond   the bounds
   of words

in this   darkness
of   our lives
the primitive in me
it   feels
without   tribe
without   fire

in that   blindness
we find   nihilism
that tribes   and tribalism
were greater   than this
modern   world

and less   than this
that came   before
this yearning for dark ages
once ruled   by myth

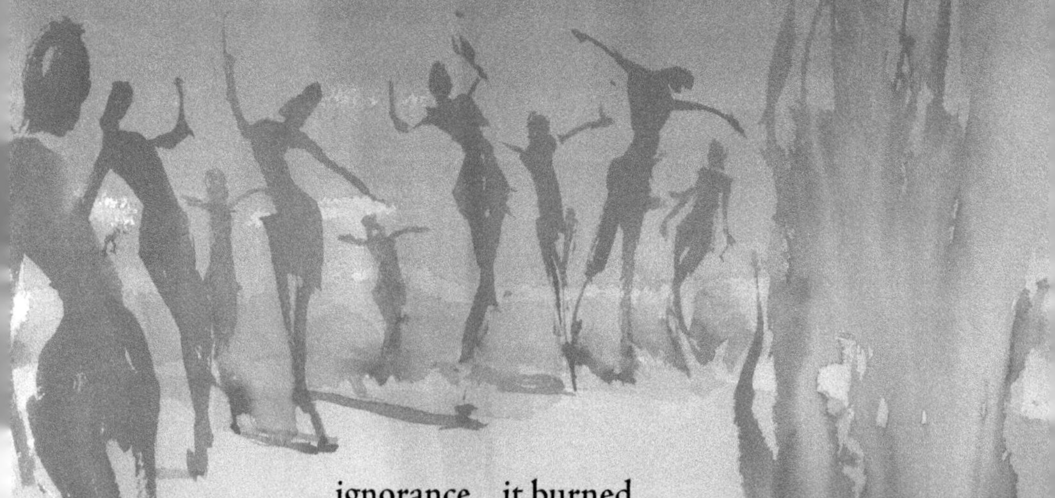

ignorance   it burned
the   world
we sacked   rome's ruins
the library   of alexandria
now   ashes

the loss   of history
the curse   of curiosity
pandora's box   unleashed
this age   of monsters

we now   believe
in   the knight
those   who slew
those   who ruled
what   we are
without   the light

unseen songs
they rule

us all

the cricket choir
such is desire

each chirp misleading
our feelings conspire

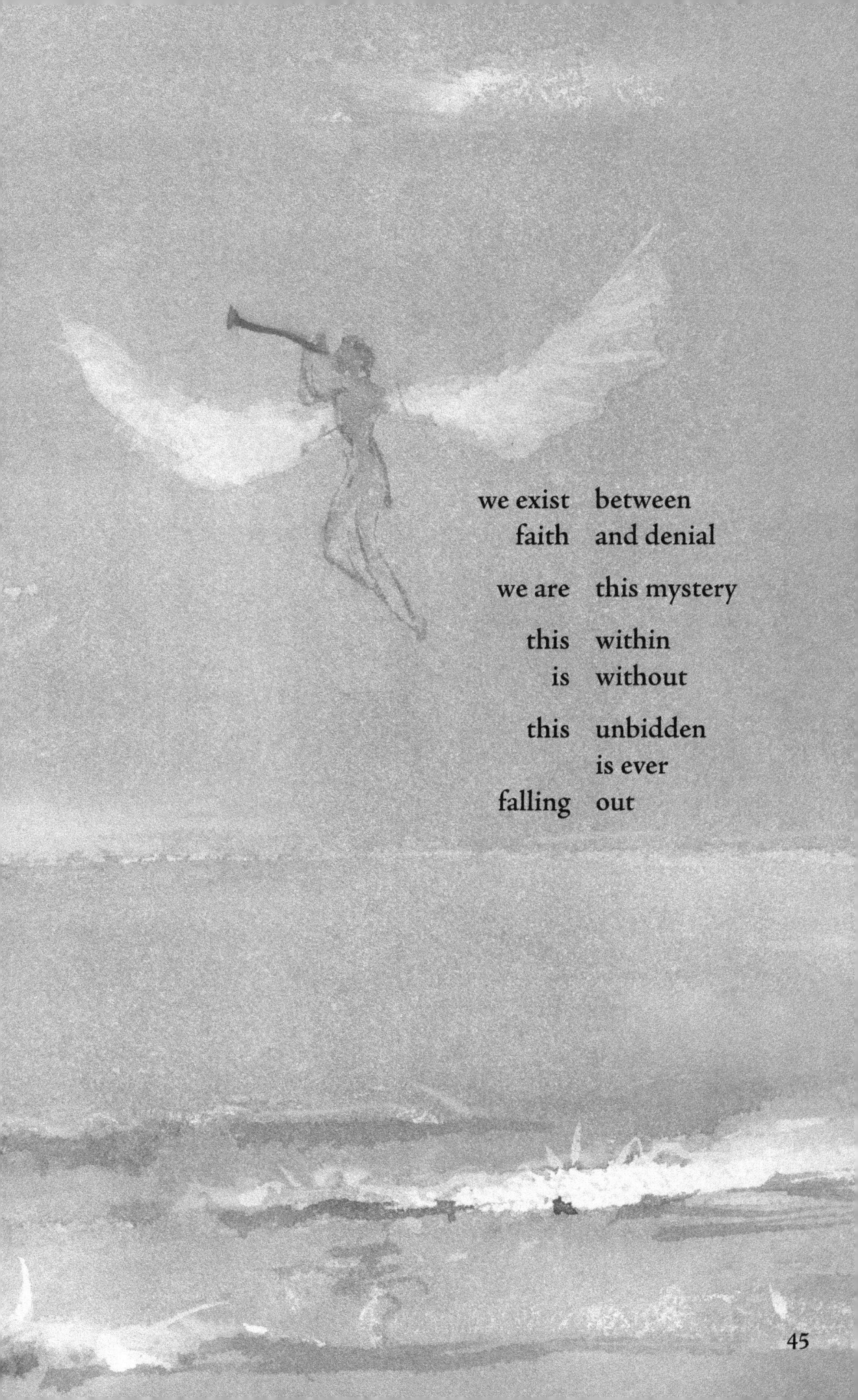

we exist   between
   faith   and denial

we are   this mystery

   this   within
     is   without

   this   unbidden
           is ever
falling   out

newton   only knew
of   falling here
only that   his apple
fell   to earth

all matter   from the flea
to the dust   of stars
that   make us
it argues   with newton's
law

we bend   the fabric
of both   space
and time
by just   existing

all   that is

every   speck

all   that be

every atom   exerts
its weight

its mass   is felt
upon   the weight
of you   and me

it is infinite   that sings
thru all   the universe
the unsingable   song
that   touches me
in   gravity

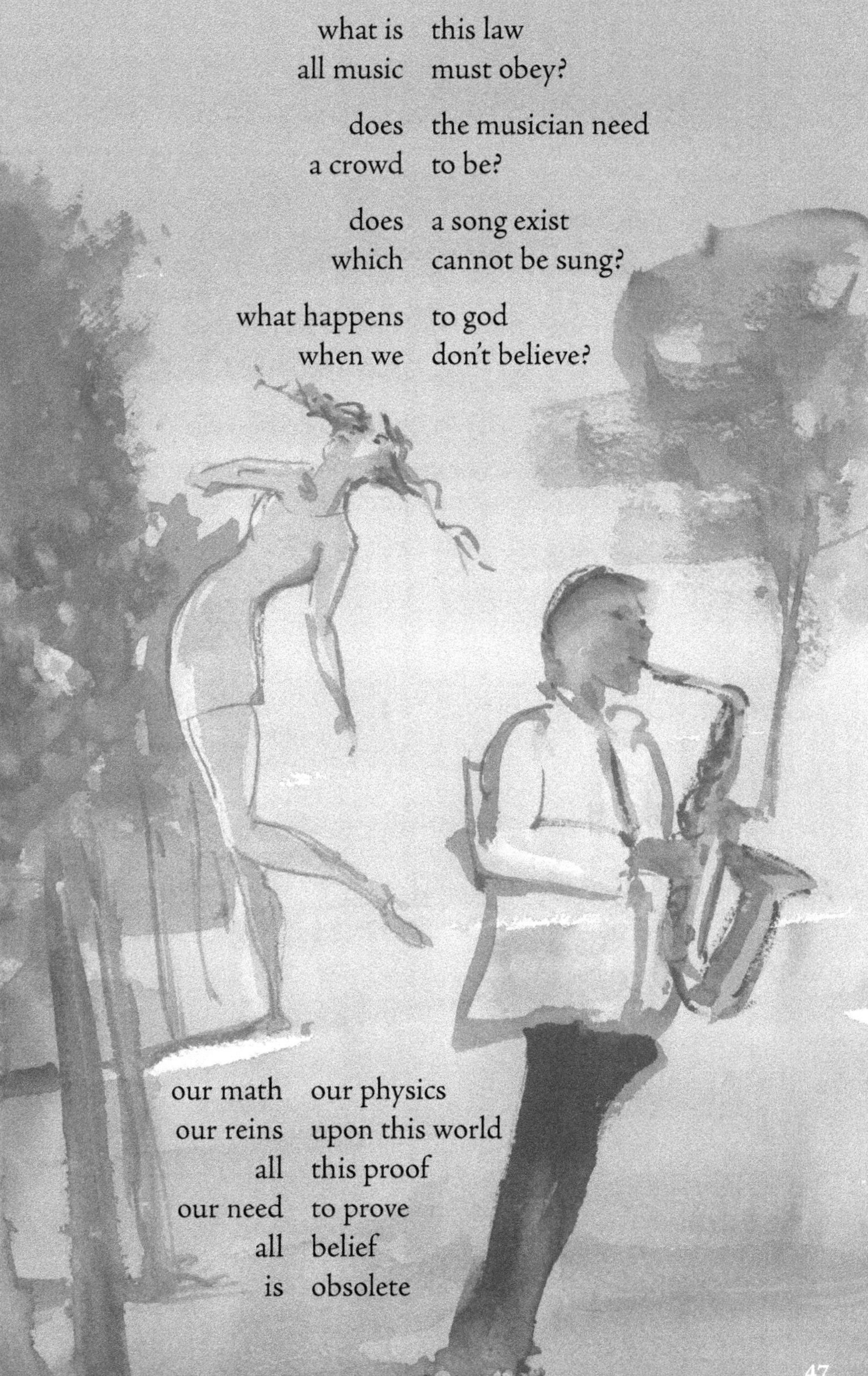

what is   this law
all music   must obey?

does   the musician need
a crowd   to be?

does   a song exist
which   cannot be sung?

what happens   to god
when we   don't believe?

our math   our physics
our reins   upon this world
all   this proof
our need   to prove
all   belief
is   obsolete

I am   not me

I dream

I witness   a vision
two   driven
from the origin   of man

a memory   imprisoned
in waking   I feel it fading
a dream   that cannot
survive   the light

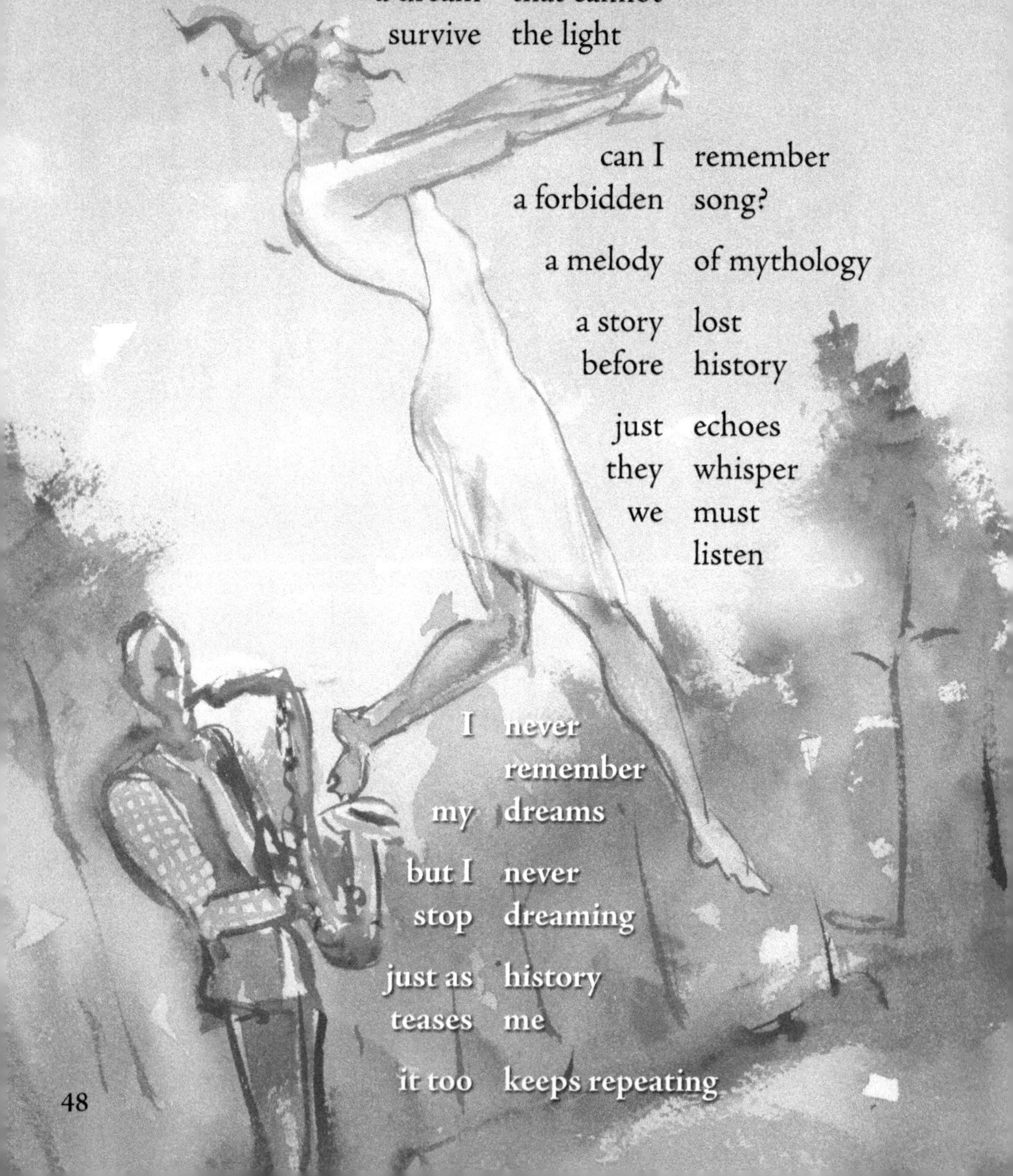

can I   remember
a forbidden   song?

a melody   of mythology

a story   lost
before   history

just   echoes
they   whisper
we   must
listen

I   never
remember
my   dreams

but I   never
stop   dreaming

just as   history
teases   me

it too   keeps repeating

this confusion   having just
                 awoken
          am I   adam?
          am I   eve?
       was this   a dream?
       was this   a remembering
            of   forbidden things?

      the first   father
      the first   mother
      the first   to feel
          that   shame
       to carry   that blame

   the whispers   of ancestors
      the terror   of angels
     the trauma   below
        the tree   of life

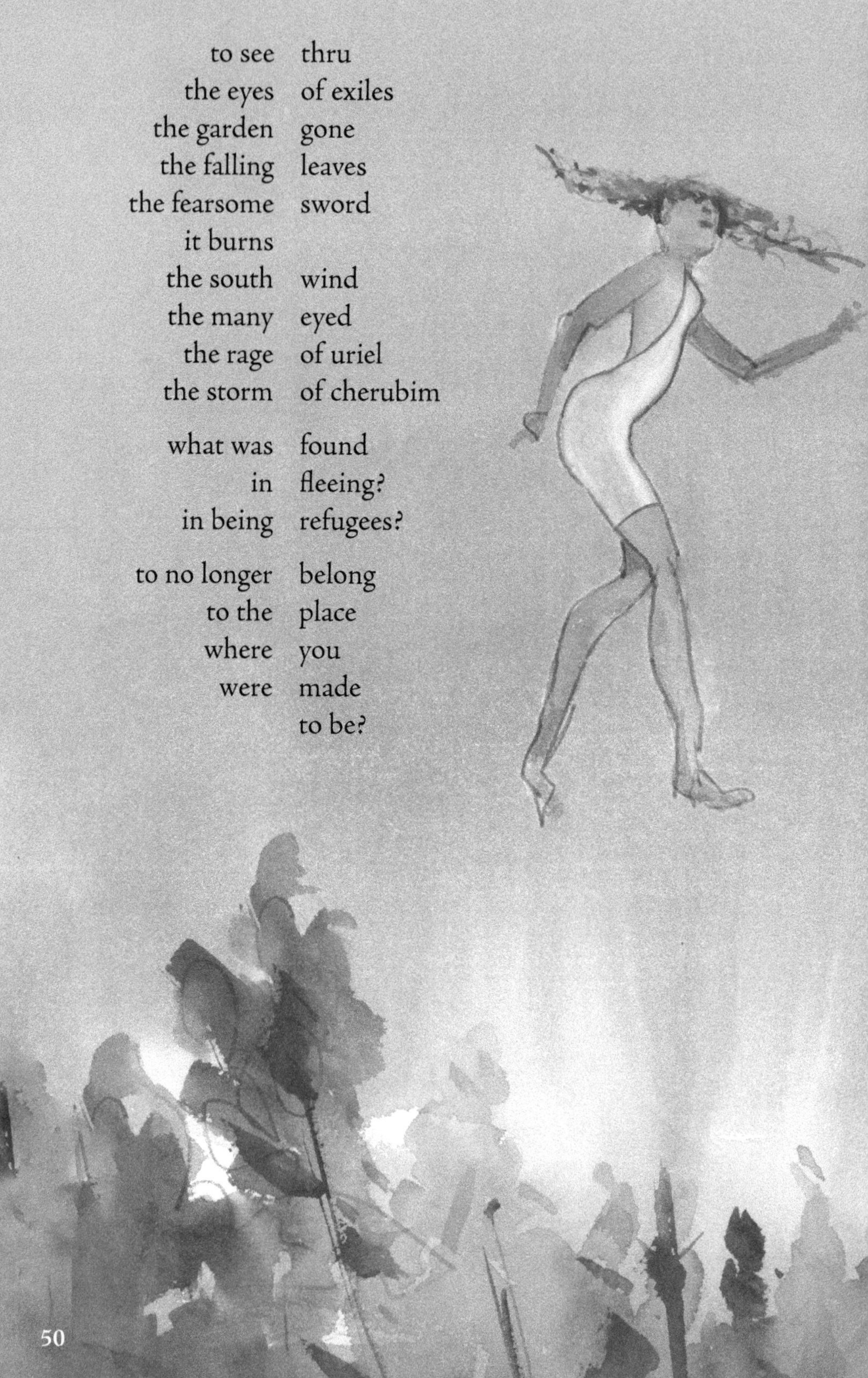
to see   thru
the eyes   of exiles
the garden   gone
the falling   leaves
the fearsome   sword
it burns
the south   wind
the many   eyed
the rage   of uriel
the storm   of cherubim

what was   found
in   fleeing?
in being   refugees?

to no longer   belong
to the   place
where   you
were   made
to be?

what caused   our fall?

was that myth   real?

did we serve   our greed?

what price   desire?

we had   everything
except   what was forbidden

yet we   needed more

the serpent   tempts
not with   apples
but with   a promise
the control   of paradise

this god   we fear
he banished   us
from   mythology
from   that garden
made just   for us

we redefined   utopia
a new ideal   monopia
just   for us
never   them
for your   eye
and   ear alone
that only   we
meaning   me
own this   monotone

never   for the fallen
never   to sing
with strangers
never   in key
never   to unlock
that garden gate
to be   that choir
that god   requires

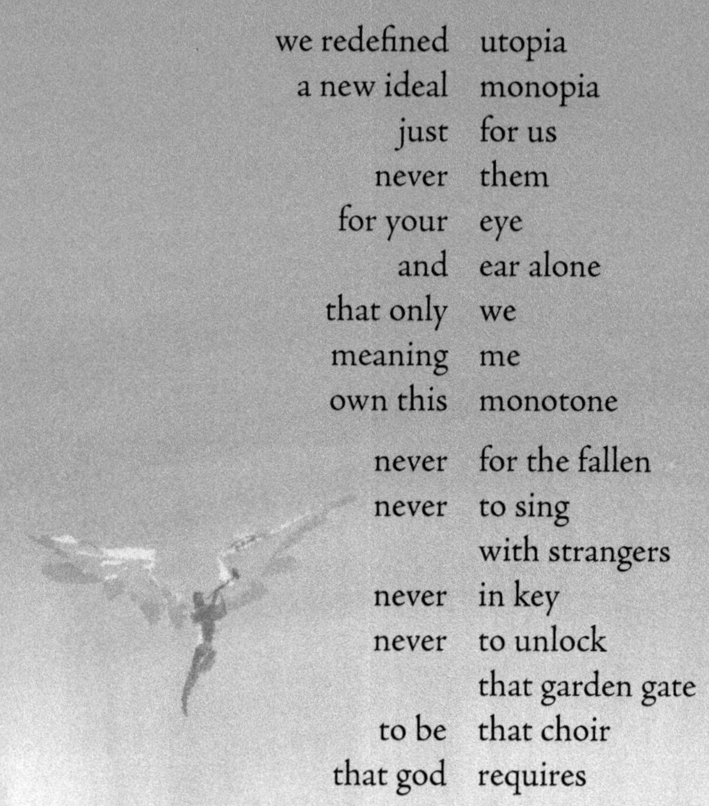

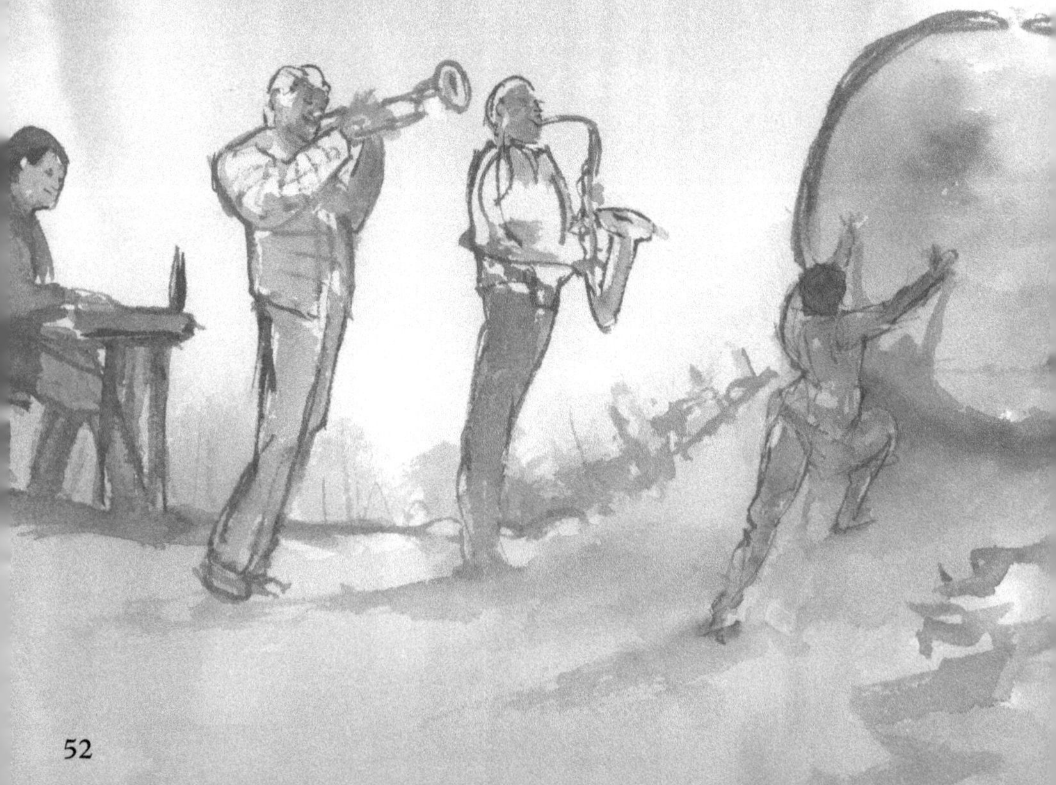

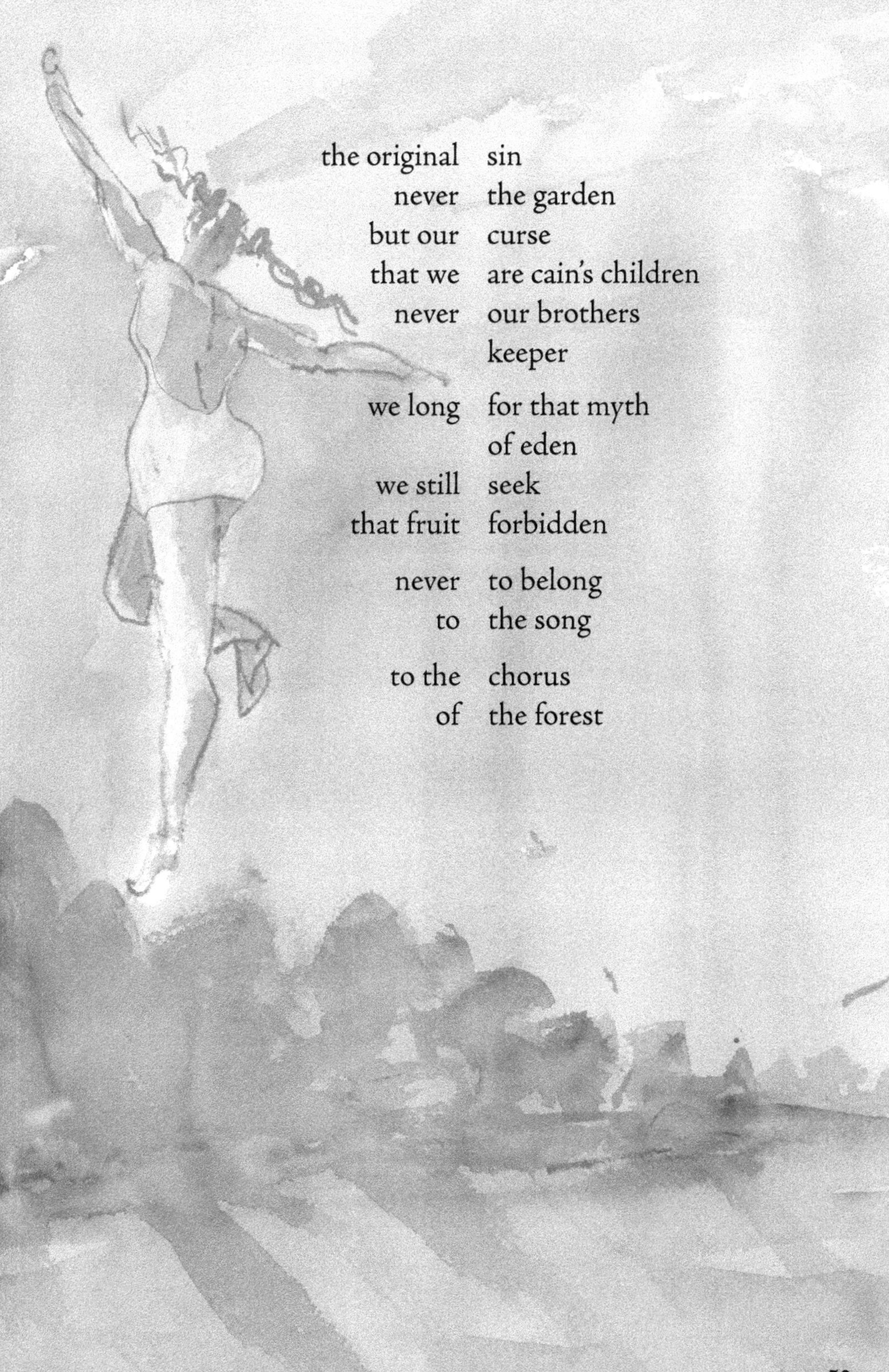

the original sin
never the garden
but our curse
that we are cain's children
never our brothers
keeper

we long for that myth
of eden
we still seek
that fruit forbidden

never to belong
to the song

to the chorus
of the forest

amongst the heavens
crowned with clouds
the thousand thousand angels
sing a song never heard
by mortal ear

but

listen

below

your noise

in that

depth

only found

in solitude

what stirs within
each silent word
of inward prayer

where
the unhearable
is heard

in each quiet
in all stillness

all existence rings

even nature sings

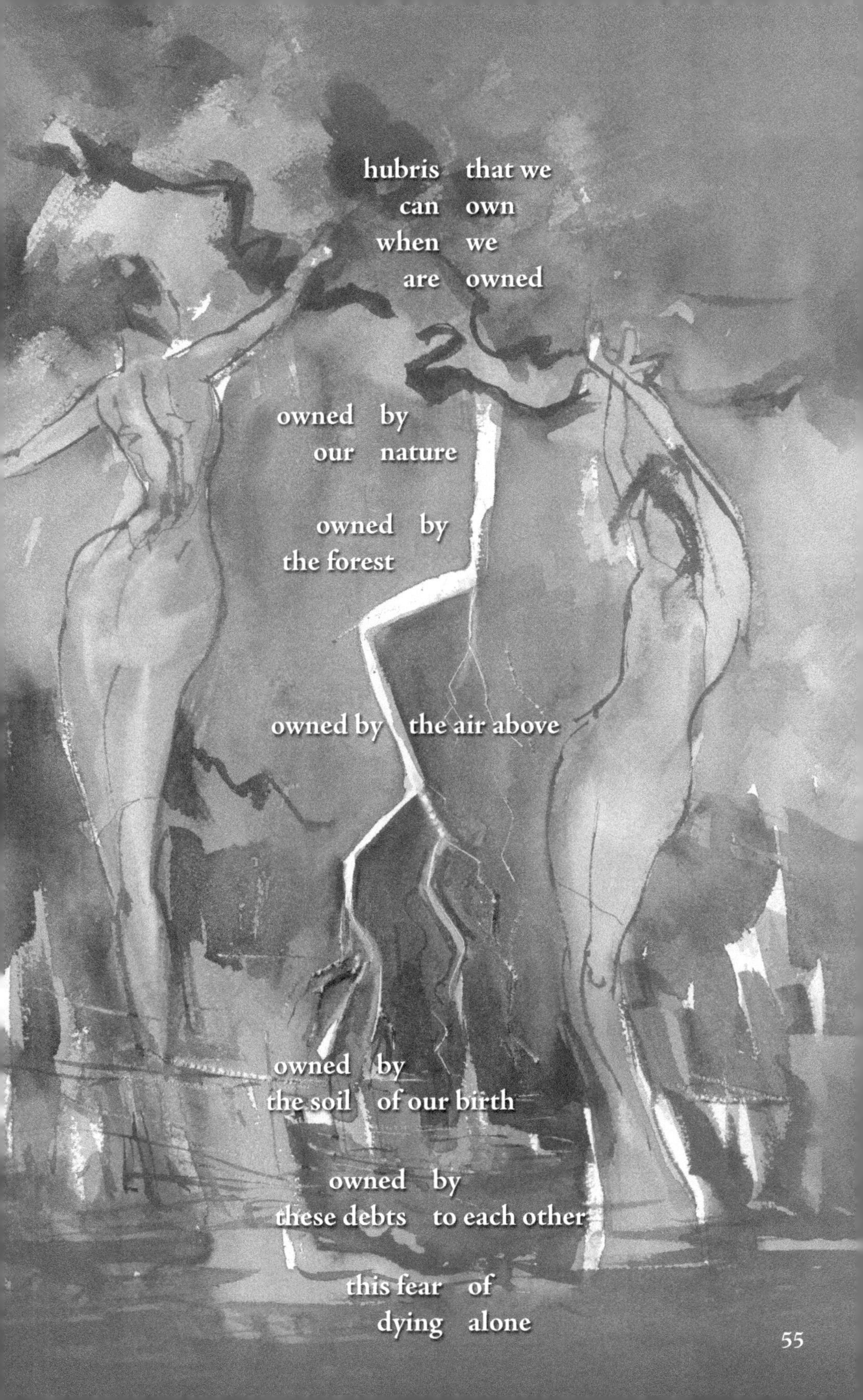

hubris   that we
                    can   own
                    when   we
                    are   owned

owned   by
our   nature

owned   by
the forest

owned by   the air above

owned   by
the soil   of our birth

owned   by
these debts   to each other

this fear   of
dying   alone

is all   existence
          subject
to these five senses?

to being observed?

to being seen?

is joining   the heard
the only proof you be?

what we   observe
what we   think
each word we choose

does not   define
but is   defined
by that   world
outside   our mind

and yet
delusions rule

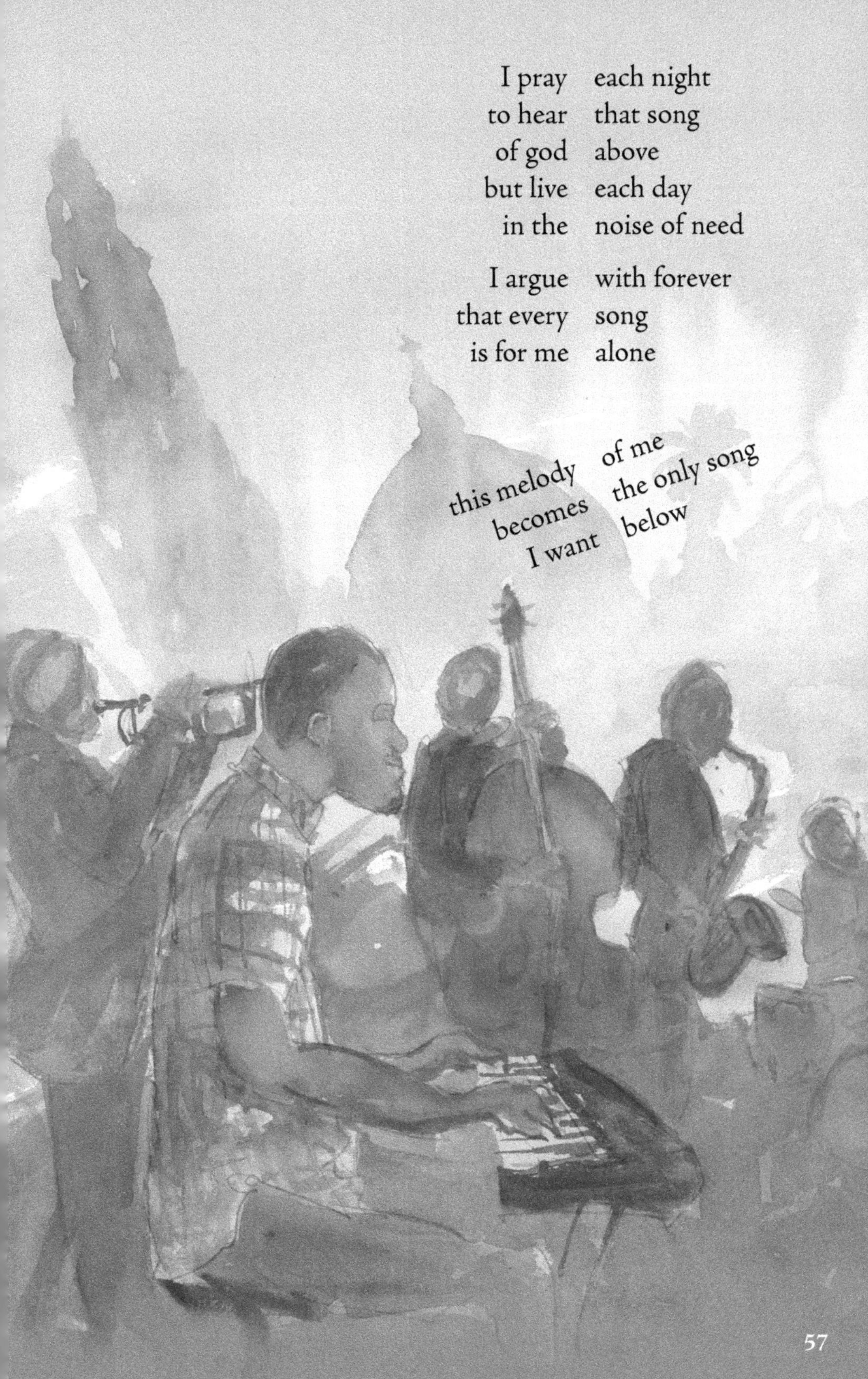

I pray   each night
to hear   that song
of god   above
but live   each day
in the   noise of need

I argue   with forever
that every   song
is for me   alone

this melody   of me
becomes   the only song
I want   below

I feud
within my senses
seeing only
what I
already believe

this feudal reign
over reality
demanding of god
his fealty
that this god
can only be
what I
believe

I can only hear
what I already know
my refusal to serve
this mortal world below

silence
is just noise
we ignore
this heart
we hold
this me that I
no longer
know

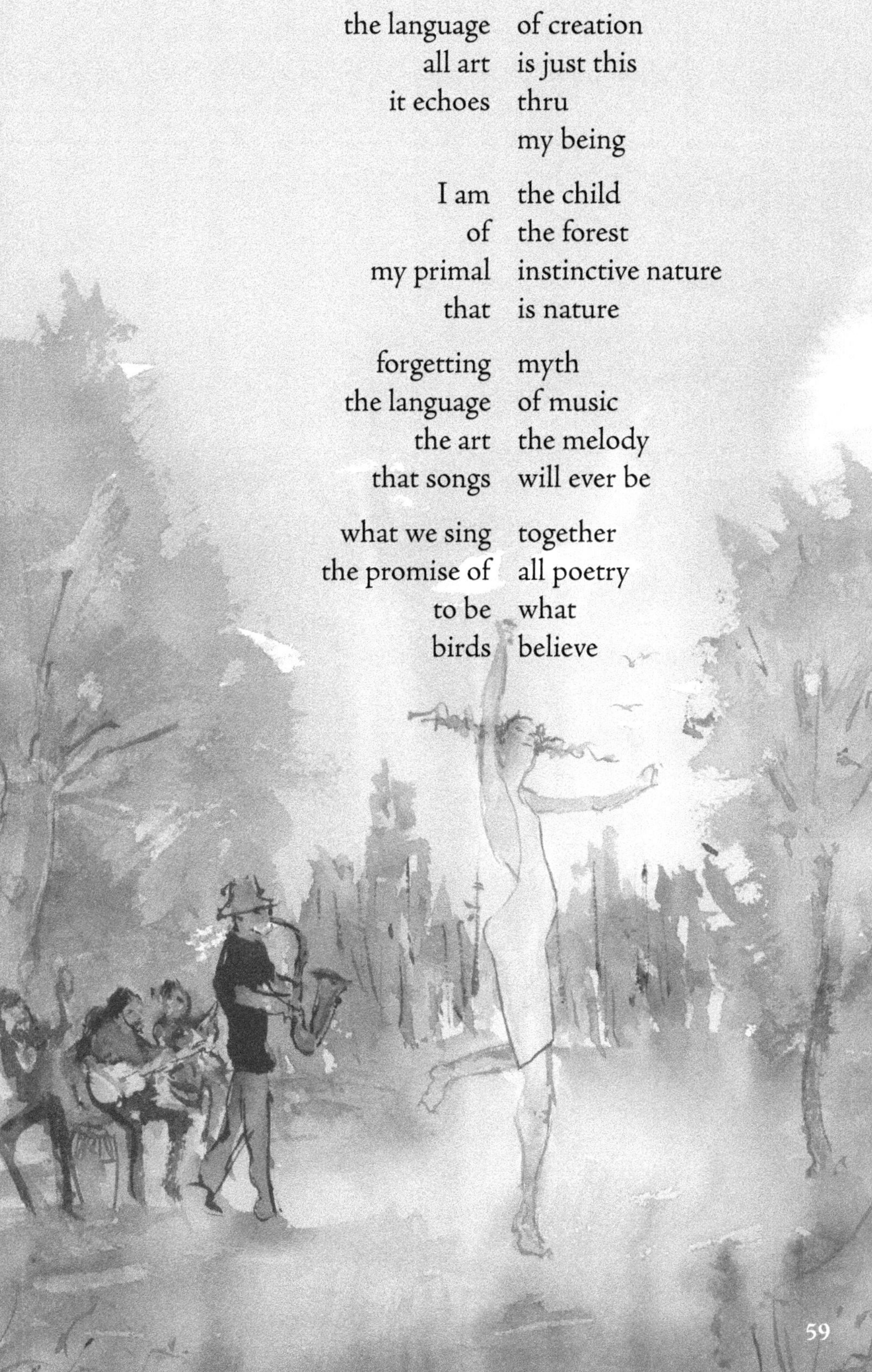

the language of creation
all art is just this
it echoes thru
my being

I am the child
of the forest
my primal instinctive nature
that is nature

forgetting myth
the language of music
the art the melody
that songs will ever be

what we sing together
the promise of all poetry
to be what
birds believe

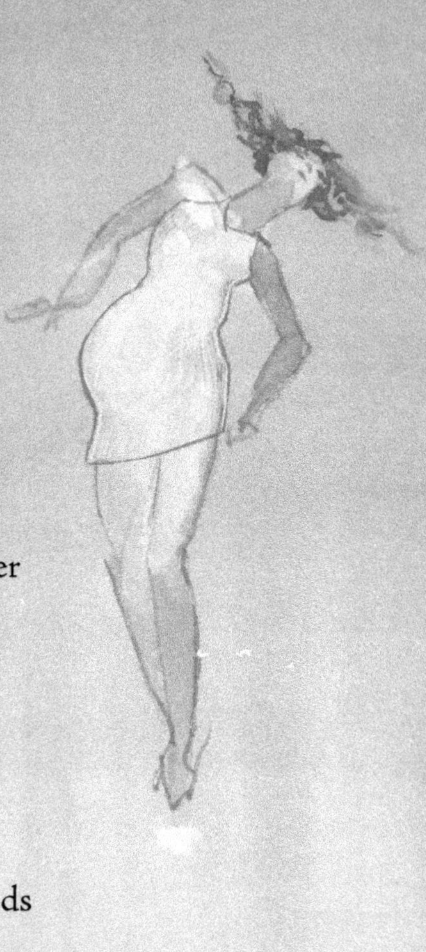

when   no prayer
has been   spoken
the drum   beat
has been   broken

when the last   believer
has   died
who still   sings
to   these gods
we've   left
          behind?

aphrodite   in her beauty
reduces us   to lust
her heart   it rules
our   thinking

athena   in her reason
wisely   studies war
as peace   will never
rule   the world

aries believes   in battle
but leaves   the fallen
to pay   their due
the wages   of war

hermes   in his speed
meets us   at our end
the messenger   of souls
will deliver us   to hade's realm

there we pay   the boatman
the wages   of our lives
his toll   these coins
we'll never   need again

as poets   mine
the depth   of words
for   power

across   millennia
what   remains

we worship   the new
never
our   foundation

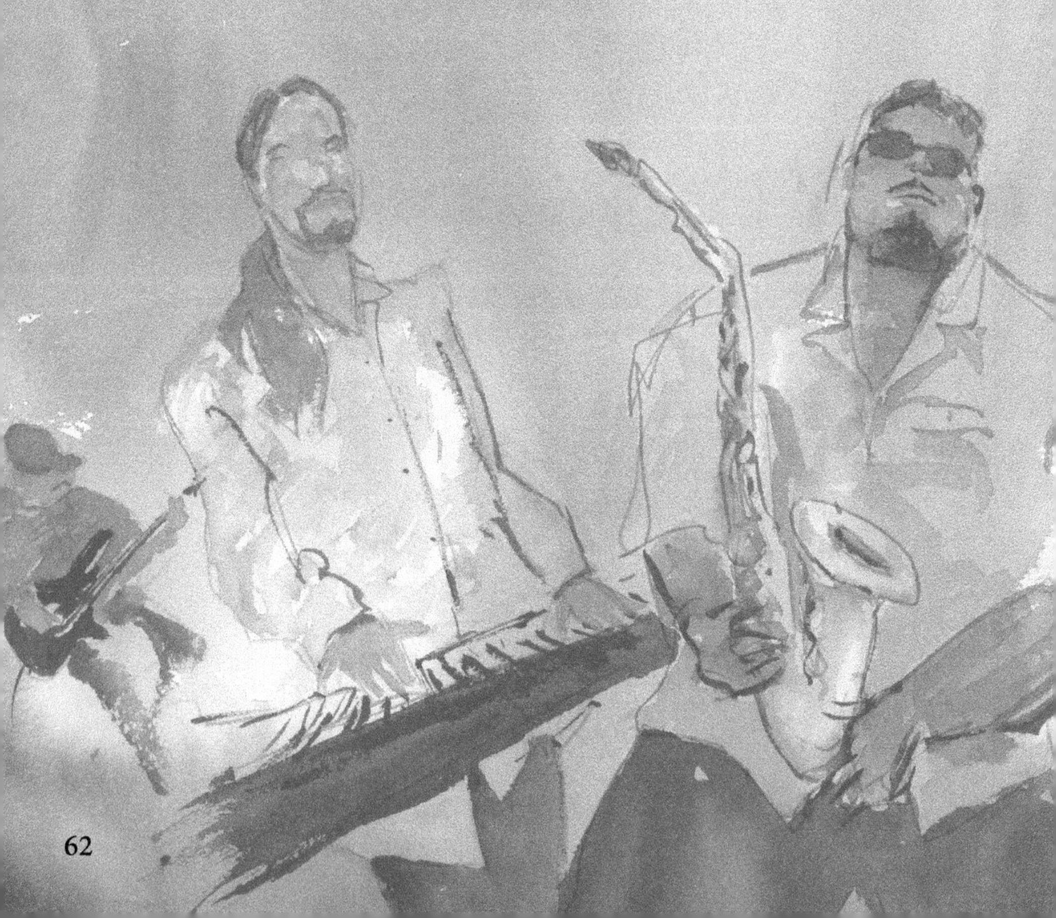

silent   is the song
of gods   forgotten
living   metaphors
of   natural laws
ideals   of man
mirrors   of
all   our flaws

we   still sing
of   olympus
fallen   not forgotten
in odes   to what was
stories   of gods
still   speaking
to what   we are

god   isn't dead
it is   mythology
the   mystery
          that died

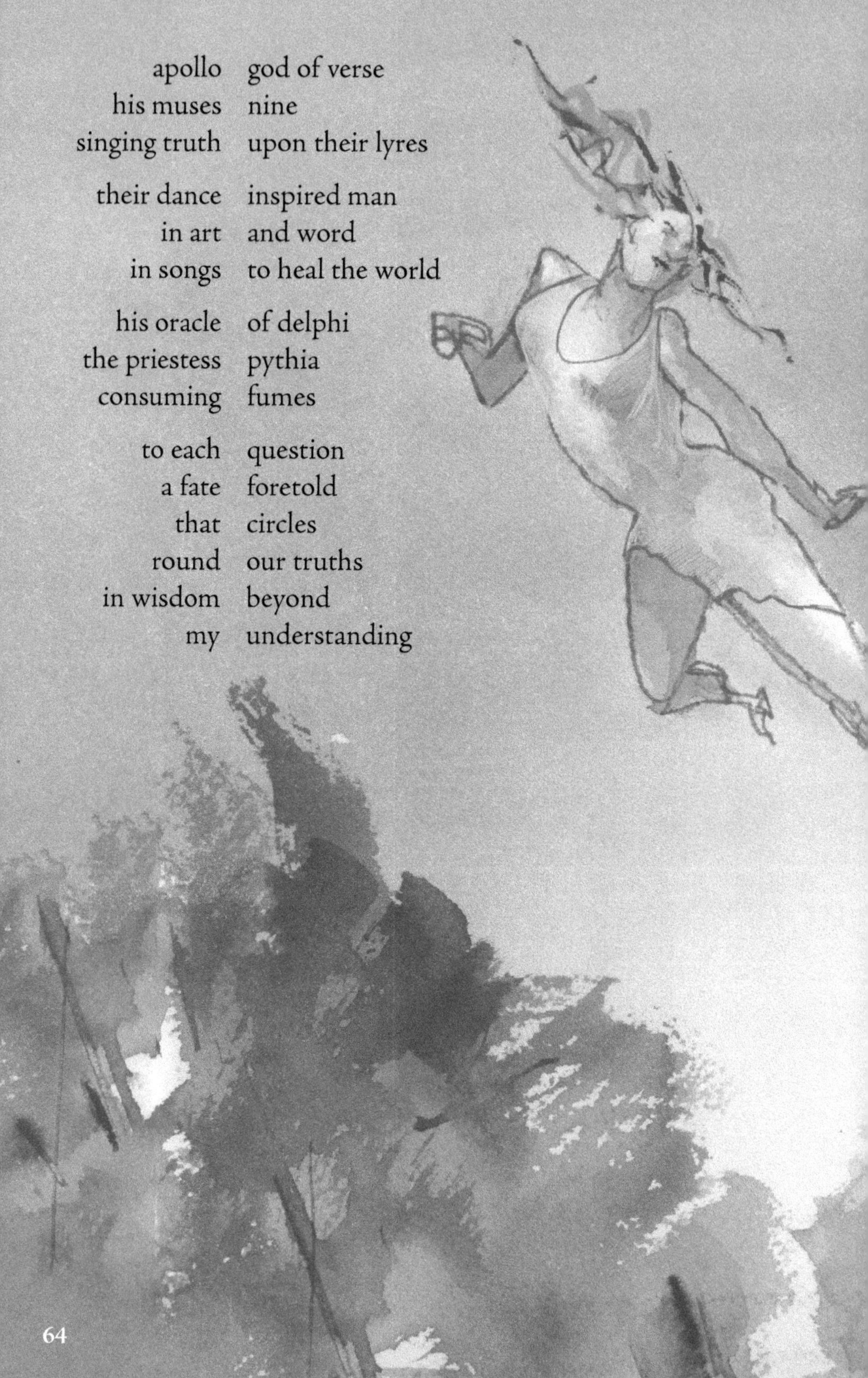

apollo   god of verse
his muses   nine
singing truth   upon their lyres

their dance   inspired man
in art   and word
in songs   to heal the world

his oracle   of delphi
the priestess   pythia
consuming   fumes

to each   question
a fate   foretold
that   circles
round   our truths
in wisdom   beyond
my   understanding

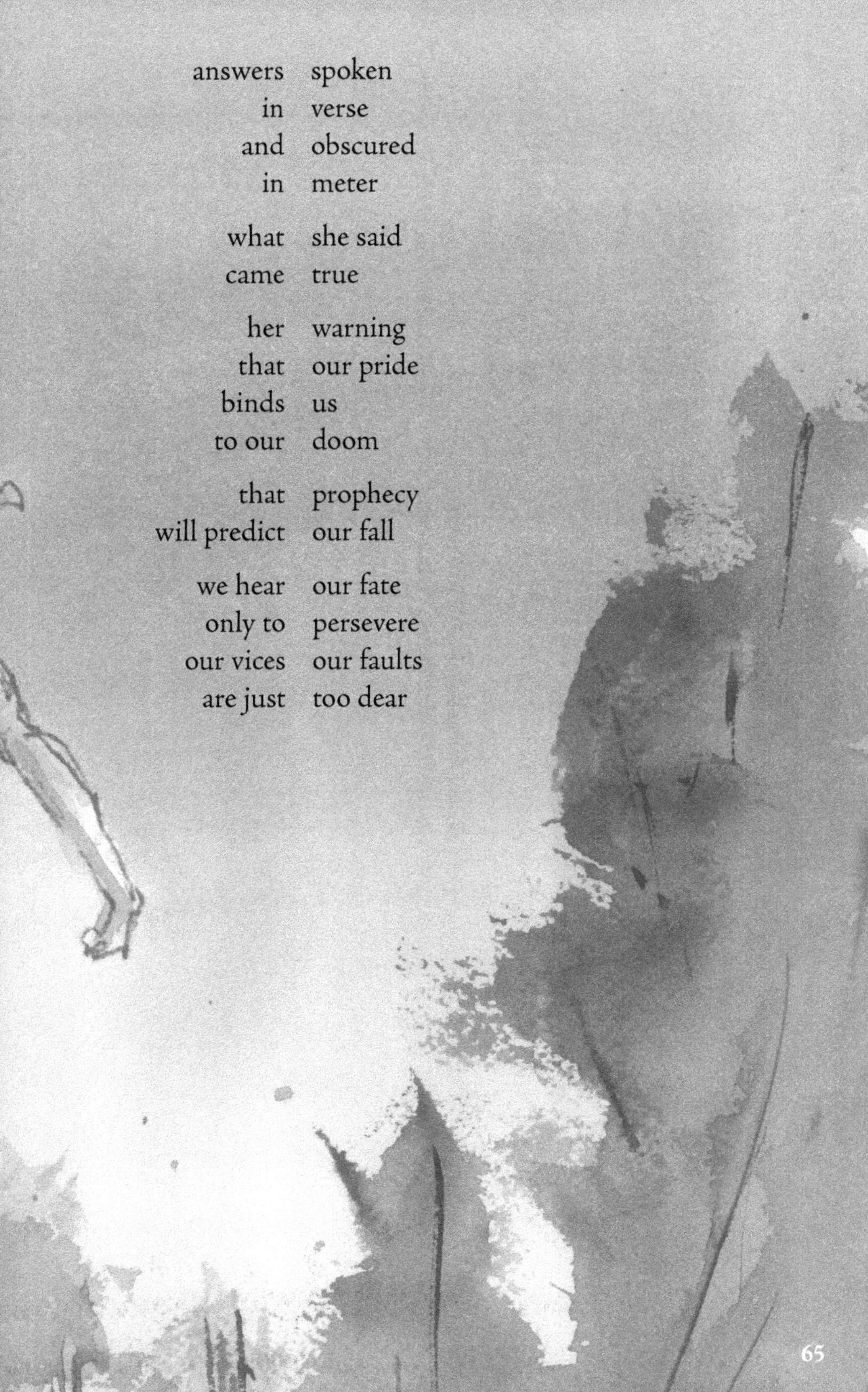

answers   spoken
in   verse
and   obscured
in   meter

what   she said
came   true

her   warning
that   our pride
binds   us
to our   doom

that   prophecy
will predict our fall

we hear   our fate
only to   persevere
our vices   our faults
are just   too dear

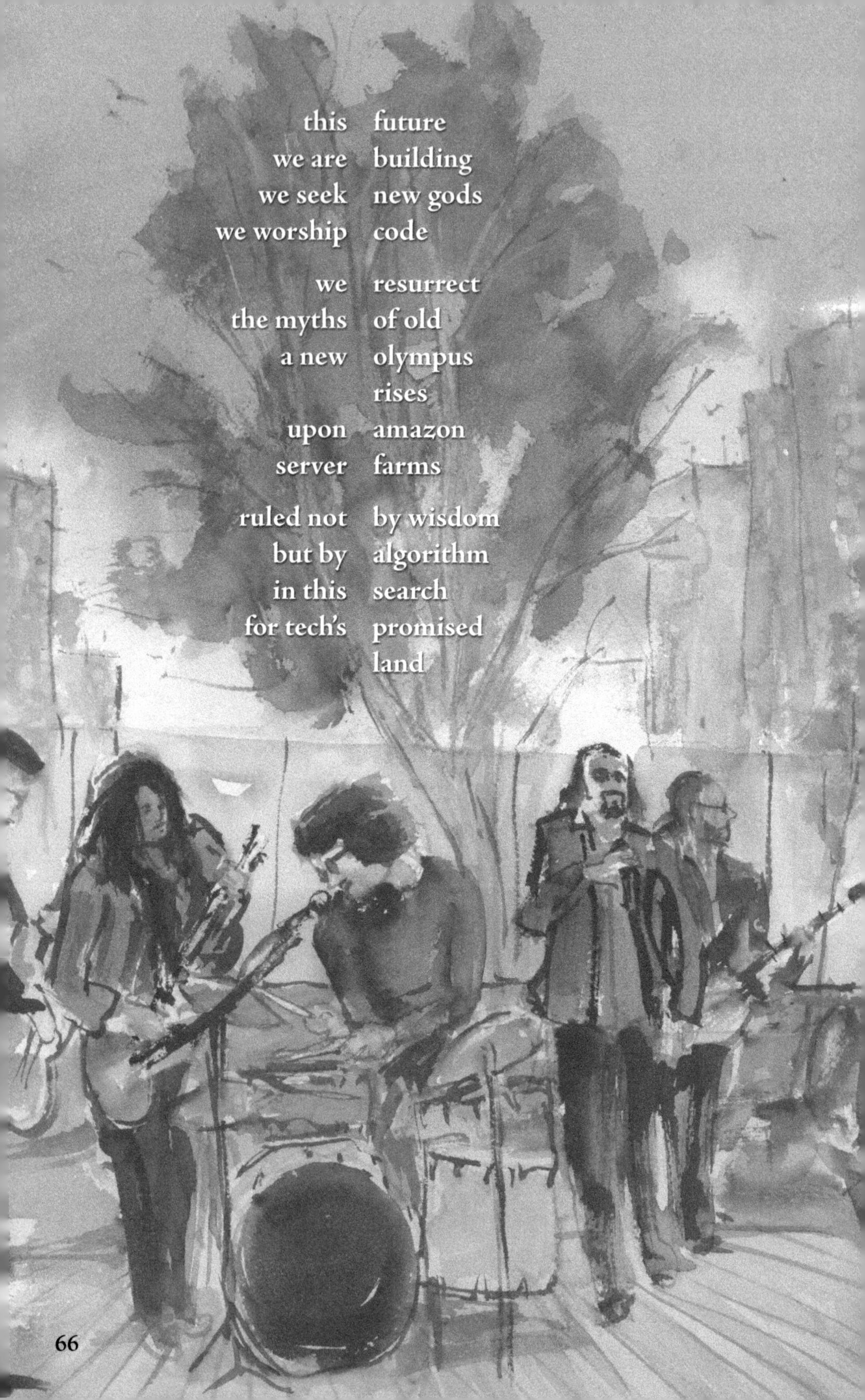

this future
we are building
we seek new gods
we worship code

we resurrect
the myths of old
a new olympus
rises
upon amazon
server farms

ruled not by wisdom
but by algorithm
in this search
for tech's promised
land

the singer
now machine
the noise of industry

the priestess   pythia
now programmed   in python

an artificial   god
a calf   of gold

the next   cash cow

apollo   now
writ   in code

a machine   that thinks
a machine   that knows
a machine   of miracles

for each   question
hallucinating   answers
the talking   spring
gurgling   generative noise

existing   only
as a   prompt
just as   god
lives   within
a prayer

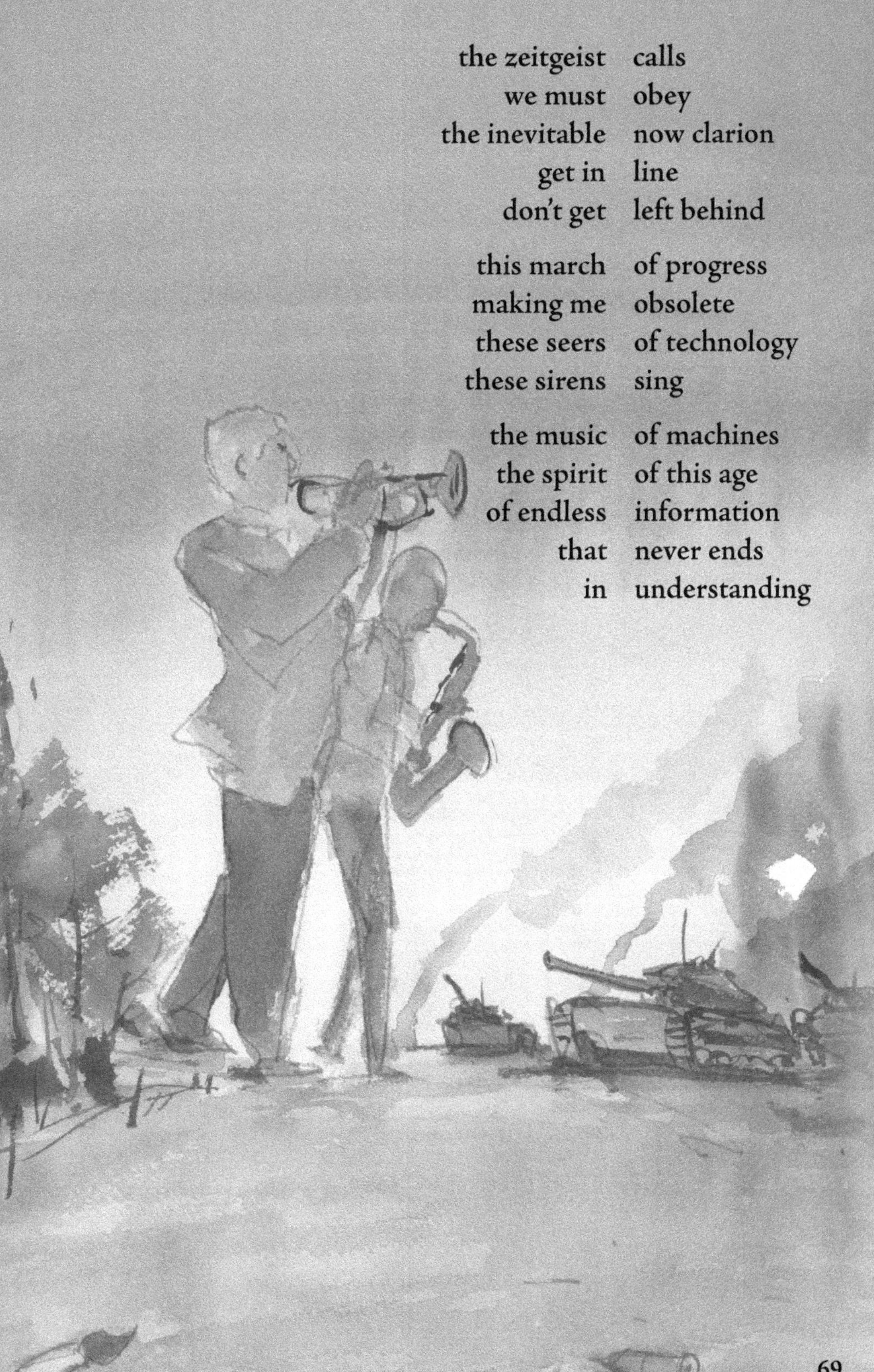

<pre>
    the zeitgeist   calls
      we must   obey
  the inevitable   now clarion
        get in   line
      don't get   left behind

     this march   of progress
    making me   obsolete
    these seers   of technology
   these sirens   sing

     the music   of machines
    the spirit   of this age
    of endless   information
          that   never ends
            in   understanding
</pre>

when did the corporation
replace all religion?

when did the altar of technology
start consuming all we are?

corporations need consumers
so they consume them

consuming all privacy
to know every thing

consuming all culture
every picture every word

consuming all our energy
the power to generate thinking

in black boxes of thought
these towers of technology
resurrecting babel
in the minds of machines

we build them
these titans of tomorrow
the monsters of myth
the eaters of gods

training on us
consuming us
made of all we are

to hack   humanity
to merge   with technology
inner lives   industrialized
community   commercialized
humanity   a commodity

we are   training data

starved   for attention
promising   perfection
selling   connection
via monthly   subscription

the degenerative   artist
a generative   model
the art   of averages
the creativity   of statistics

corporations   the makers
of faster   better and cheaper
now   creating
artificial   beings

reinventing   the plantation

replacing
all   our labor
with   the slavery
of machines

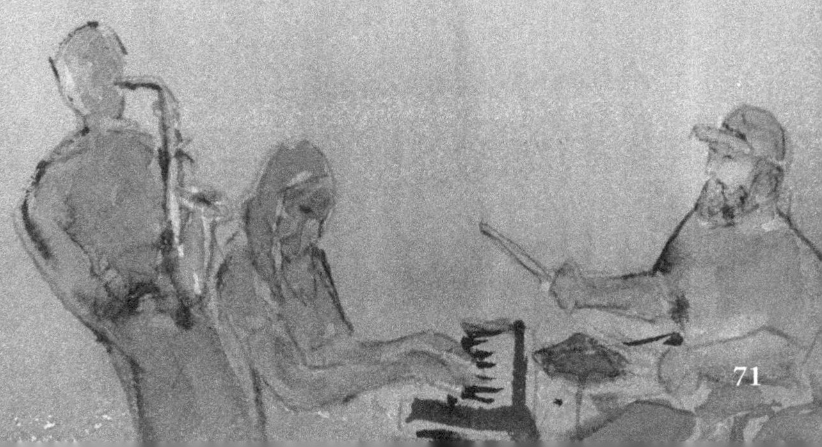

my food
it speaks to me

what I eat
what it's made of
each vitamin each mineral
compose the flavors
that sing to me

a melody of the sweet
and the sour
the bitter the salty
the umami of savory

what I miss
my body feels
my cells speak
to every unmet need
where I am deficient
it is there taste is driven

hunger arises from my nature
inner desire guides
balancing diet

this body did not evolve
in grocery stores
this drive for fast food
all convenience is packaged
against me

what I consume
man made against nature
the artificial the manufactured
engineered flavors that mimic need
yet empty of anything

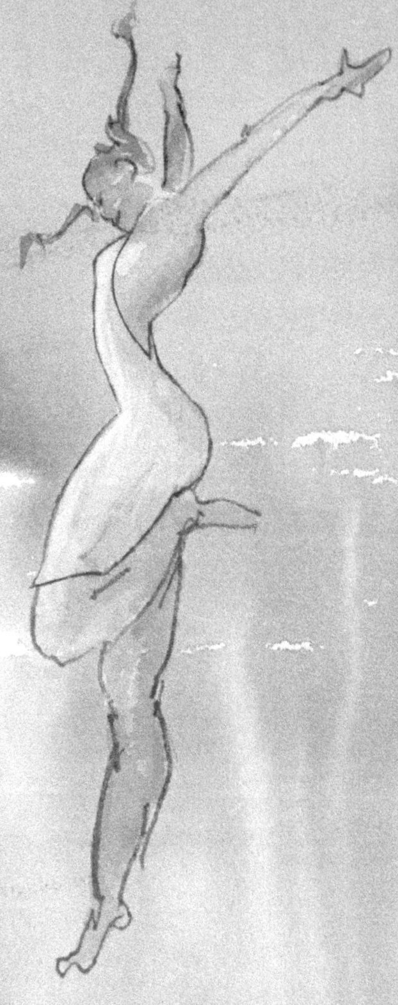

my body confused
never finding what I need
it cannot adapt
it doubles down
I eat more and more

I know that flavor
what it hides
what it must be hiding
in that next bite
my stomach sings
a song unheard
a diet of desire
not balanced from within
but from without

from what I watch
jingles repeating bells ringing
salivating to the noise
of marketing
this is not addiction
I was never the glutton
never the sinner
never the damned of dante

in that third circle
always hungry always eating
while every bite
nothing but dust

this hunger manufactured
a feast without substance
not of nature not of the garden
nor that forbidden apple

just consumers consuming
these flavors of emptiness

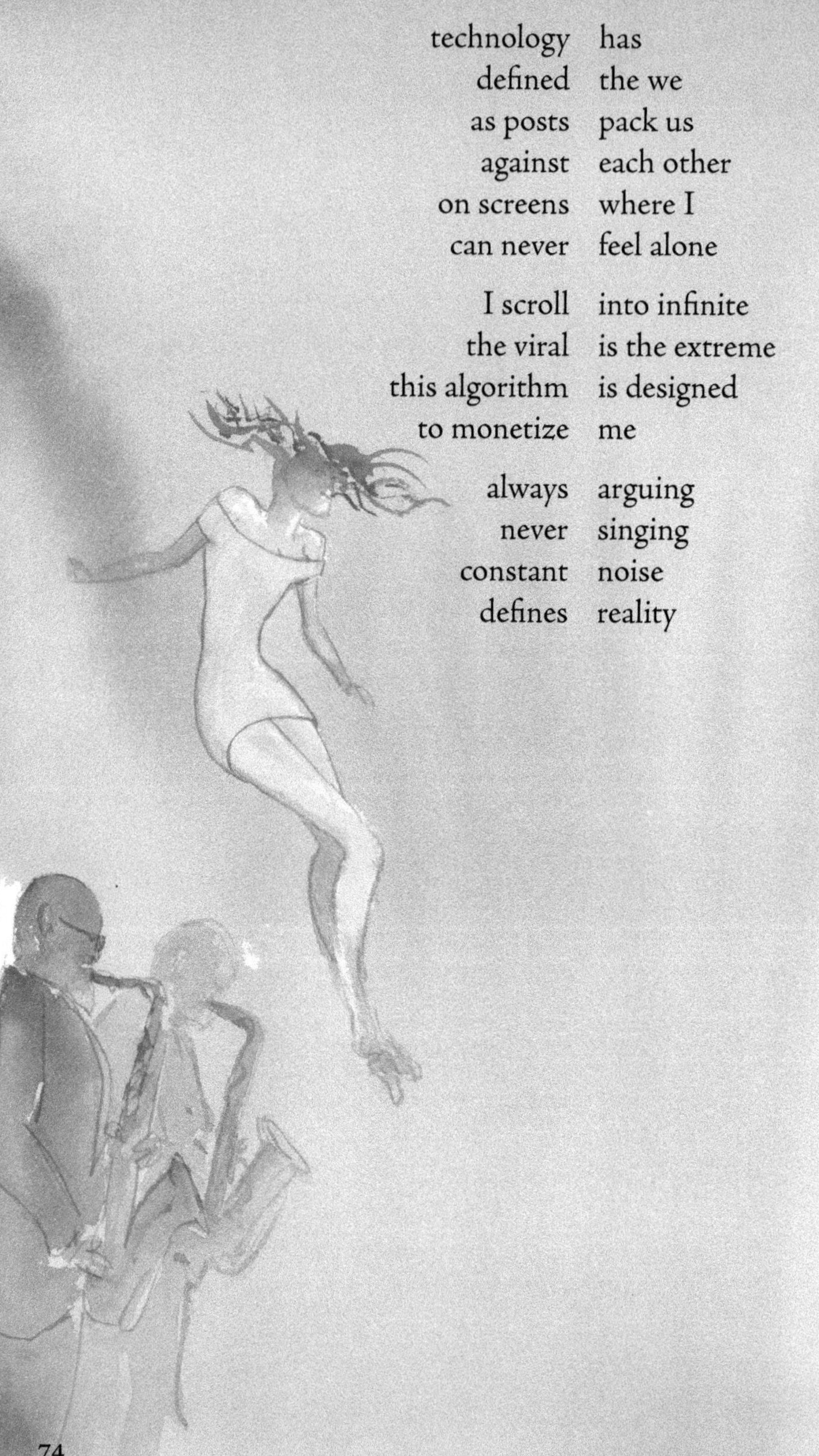

technology   has
defined   the we
as posts   pack us
against   each other
on screens   where I
can never   feel alone

I scroll   into infinite
the viral   is the extreme
this algorithm   is designed
to monetize   me

always   arguing
never   singing
constant   noise
defines   reality

your news   is never
my   news
nothing   is new
the news   now memes
that never   mean anything

within   our screens
we think   we see
all the   same things
but   my screen
and   your screen
tell   us
different   things

every screen   a universe
every head   a world
our minds   apart
this is   not division
this is   a difference
of   dimensions
in these   alternate
versions   of reality
of course   this we
can   never agree

looking   thru
this looking   glass
screens   that meet
every   need
screens   that know
every   thing
screens   designed
for   dopamine

the songs
we once   sung aloud
what once   brought us
all   together
we stream   them now

we've got   faster
we've got   cheaper
we've eliminated   the singer

we've made   the makers
of music
obsolete

just ask   for a tune
each perfect   line
auto generated   rhyme
statistics   now lyrics

with voices   they've stolen
what is real?   what is true?

the sound   without soul
better   than
any human   can do

what are   we now?

what   comes next?

what is   a song
without   a singer?

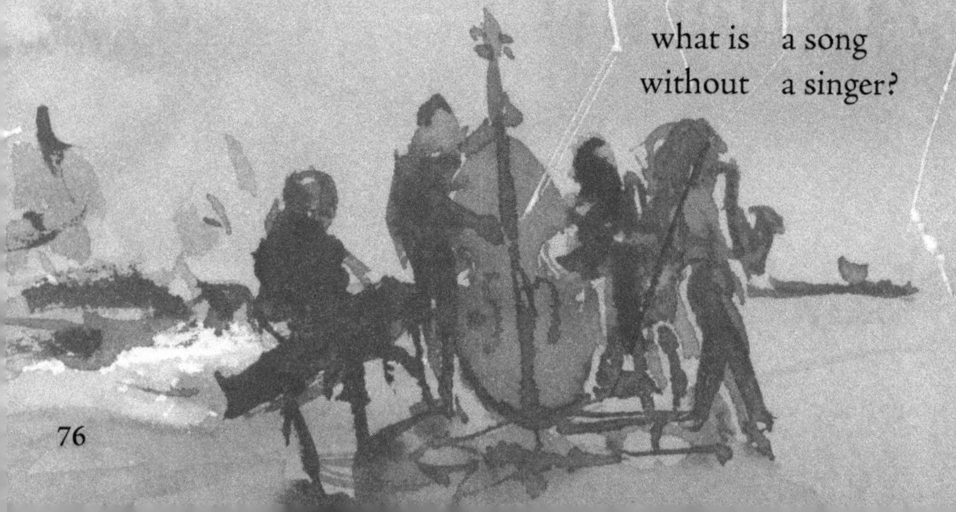

is this world　now
a　simulation?
composing　for me
a soundtrack　of isolation
our love　of things
our things　now sing

the music　of
artificial　being
making　us feel
the feelings　of machines

from voices　recorded
from　long ago

this continuous　feed
it sings　to me

what　was once
sung　aloud
what once　brought us
all　together

on headphones　all alone
I scroll　and scroll

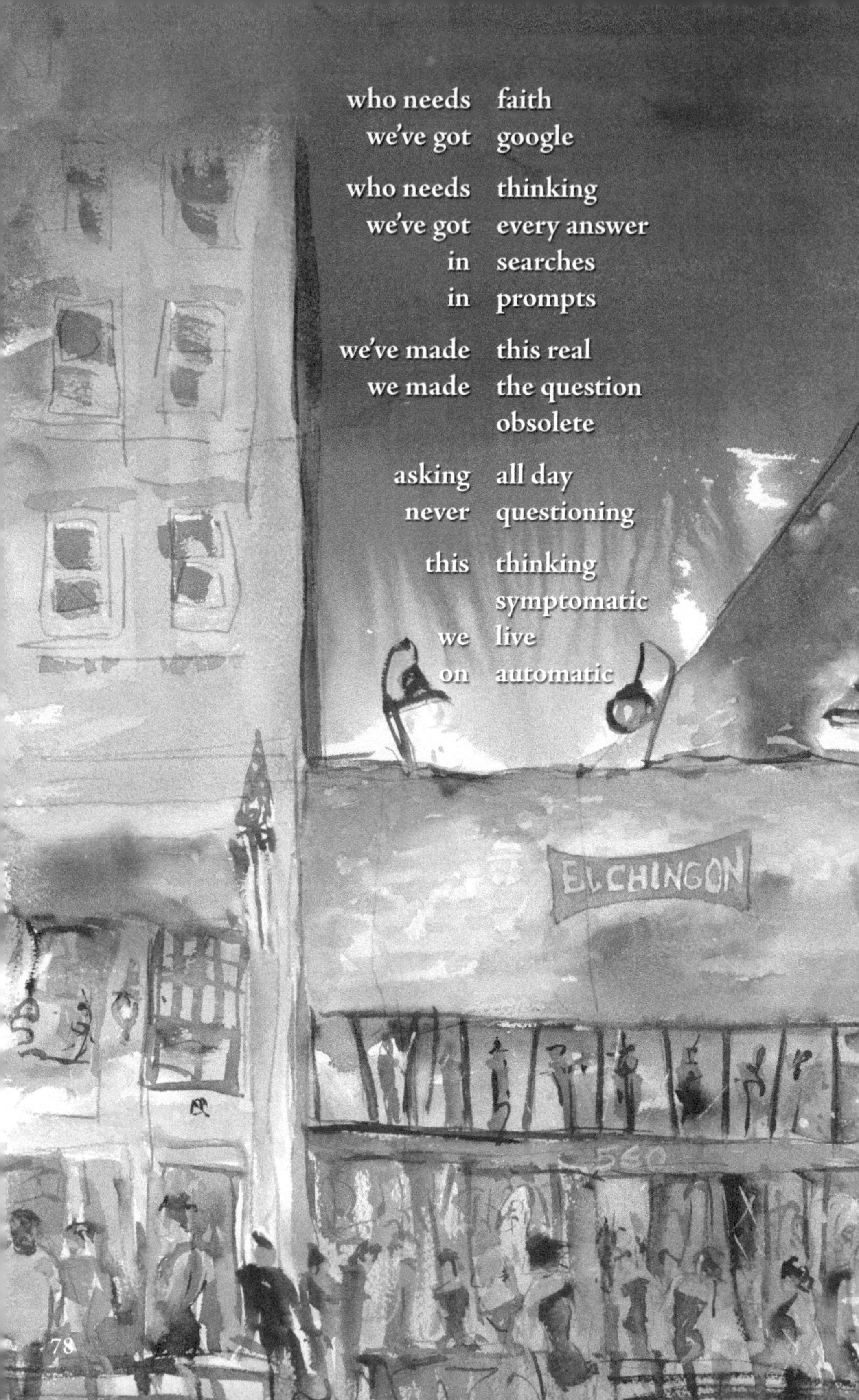

who needs   faith
we've got   google

who needs   thinking
we've got   every answer
in   searches
in   prompts

we've made   this real
we made   the question
obsolete

asking   all day
never   questioning

this   thinking
symptomatic
we   live
on   automatic

EL CHINGON
560
78

instant gratification
defines our mind
in reaction
never consideration
within our comfort
we zone out of control

born with the right of man
to wage a war
upon our soul
we lose the rights
we fail to exercise

win or lose
no matter how
hard we try
we still serve
we will cede
to destiny
we meet our time
we will die

in that still repose
what questions still?
what is this I never asked?
while I was alive?
hey google do you know?

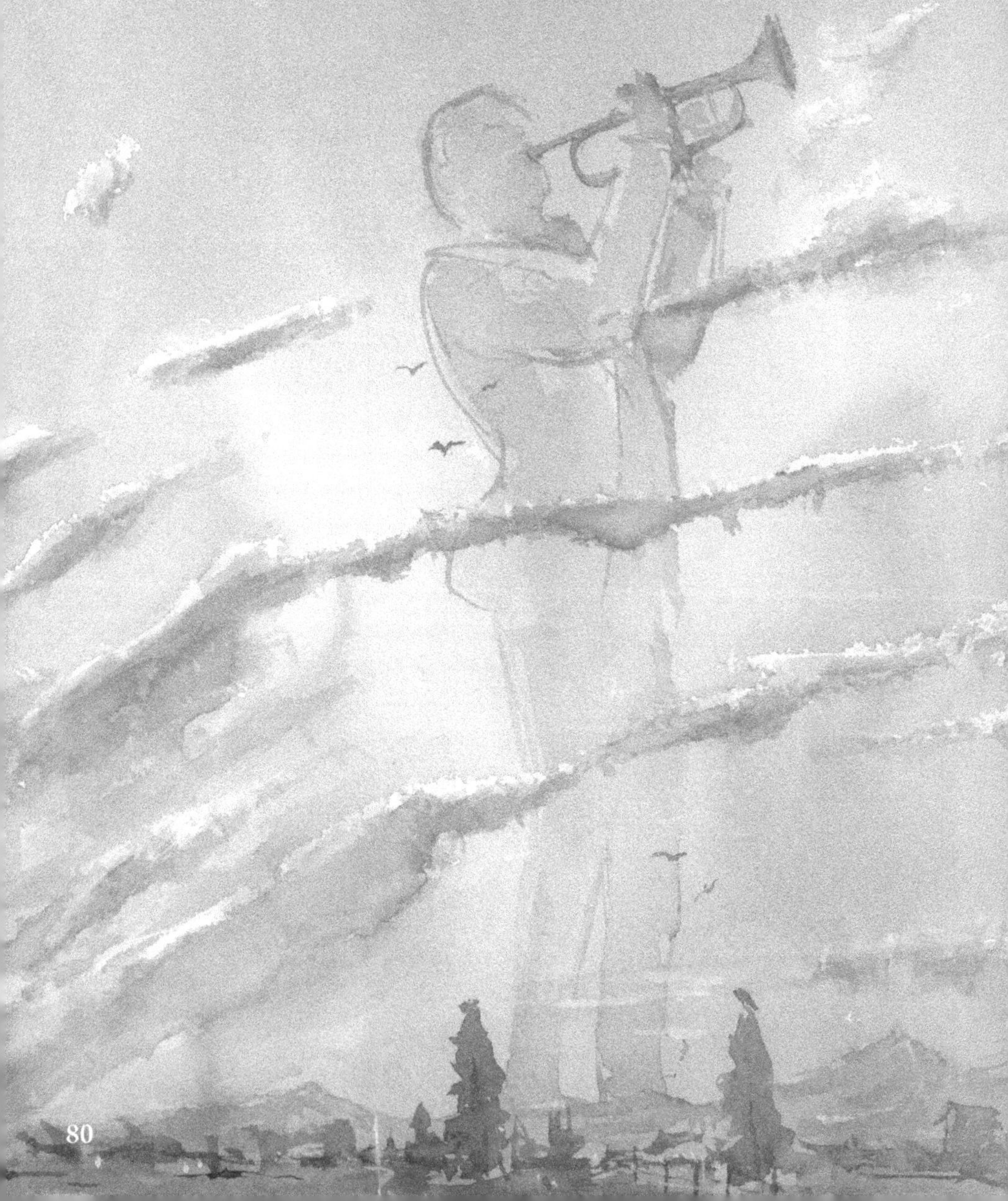

never heard   that song
              of heaven
just what   you want
              to hear
only what   you want
              to sing

is humanity   now
     writing   the song
                of nature?

 from this   tower
 we build   to god
  we can   only fall

  we are   the fallen

   I am   falling

 until I   can fall
            no more

  will I   finally feel
            the earth?

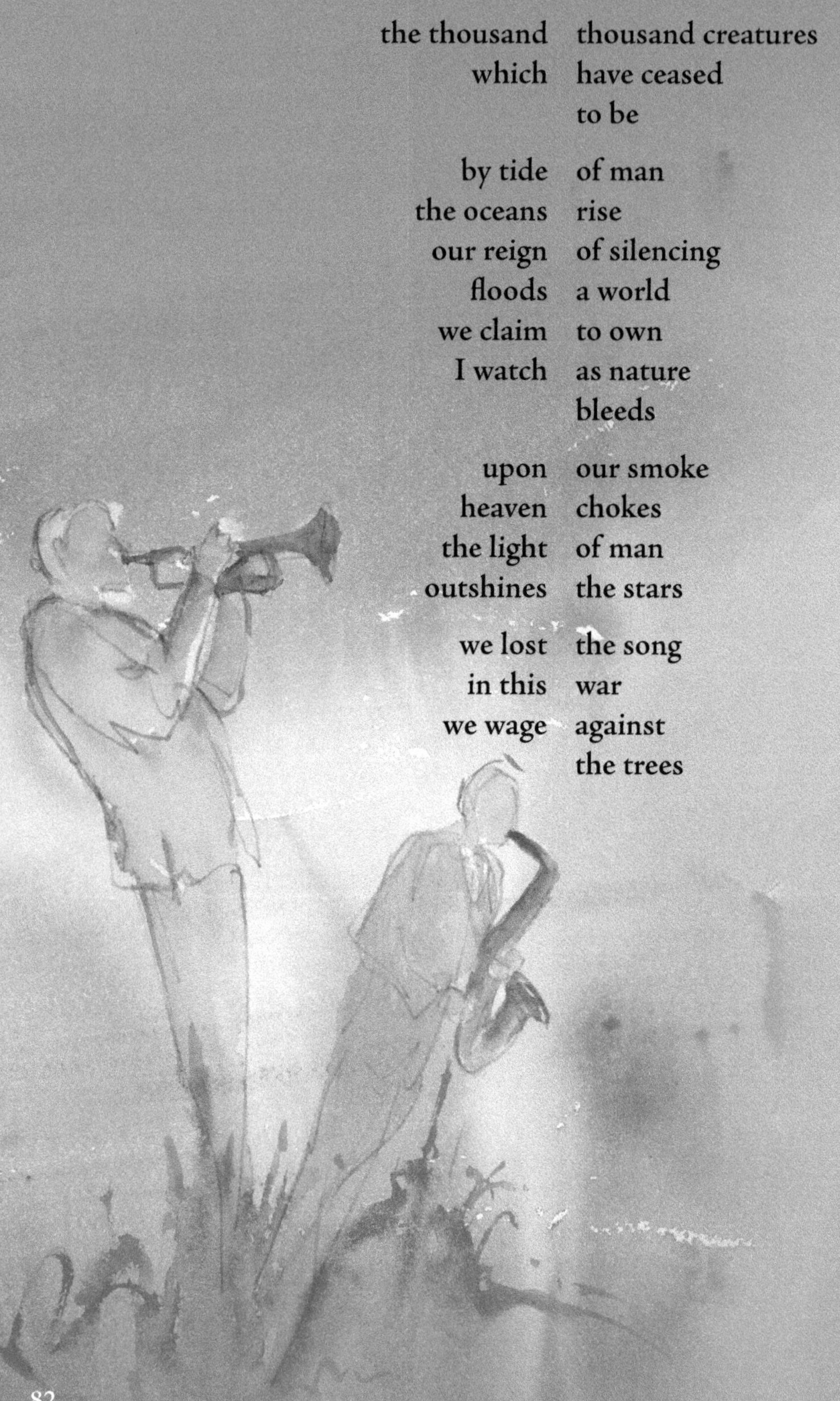

the thousand thousand creatures
which have ceased
to be

by tide of man
the oceans rise
our reign of silencing
floods a world
we claim to own
I watch as nature
bleeds

upon our smoke
heaven chokes
the light of man
outshines the stars

we lost the song
in this war
we wage against
the trees

the birds   and the
bees   are dying

the songs   and
the flowers   following

listen to   the echoes
memories   of when
heaven   and nature
sang

I am left   repeating
that song   out of tune

words   escape me
my heart   turns
against   me
each beat   striking me
blow   after blow

no song   is sadder
then   one
no longer   sung

the birds   and the
bees   are dying

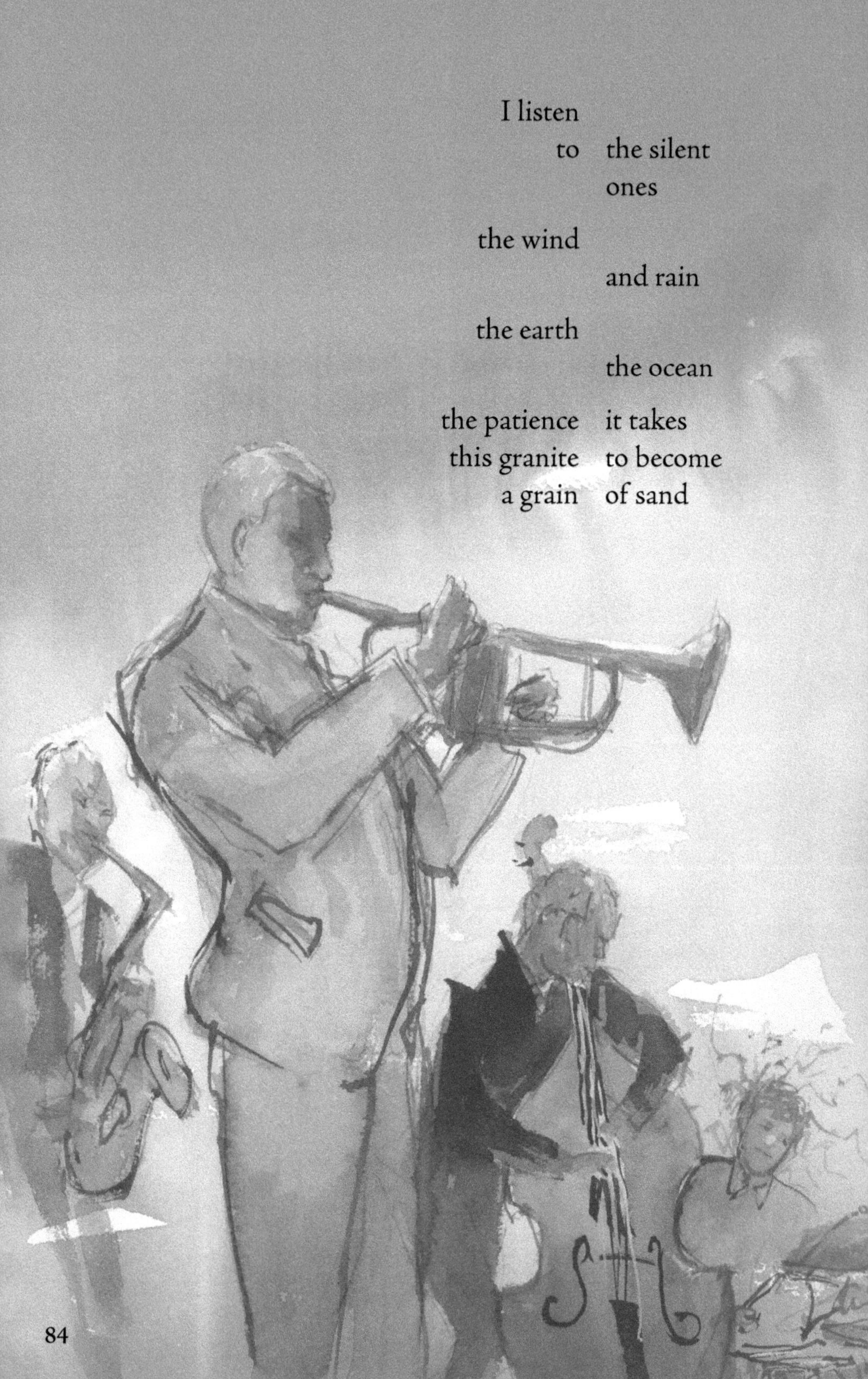

I listen
to the silent
ones
the wind
and rain
the earth
the ocean
the patience it takes
this granite to become
a grain of sand

the singers
of silence

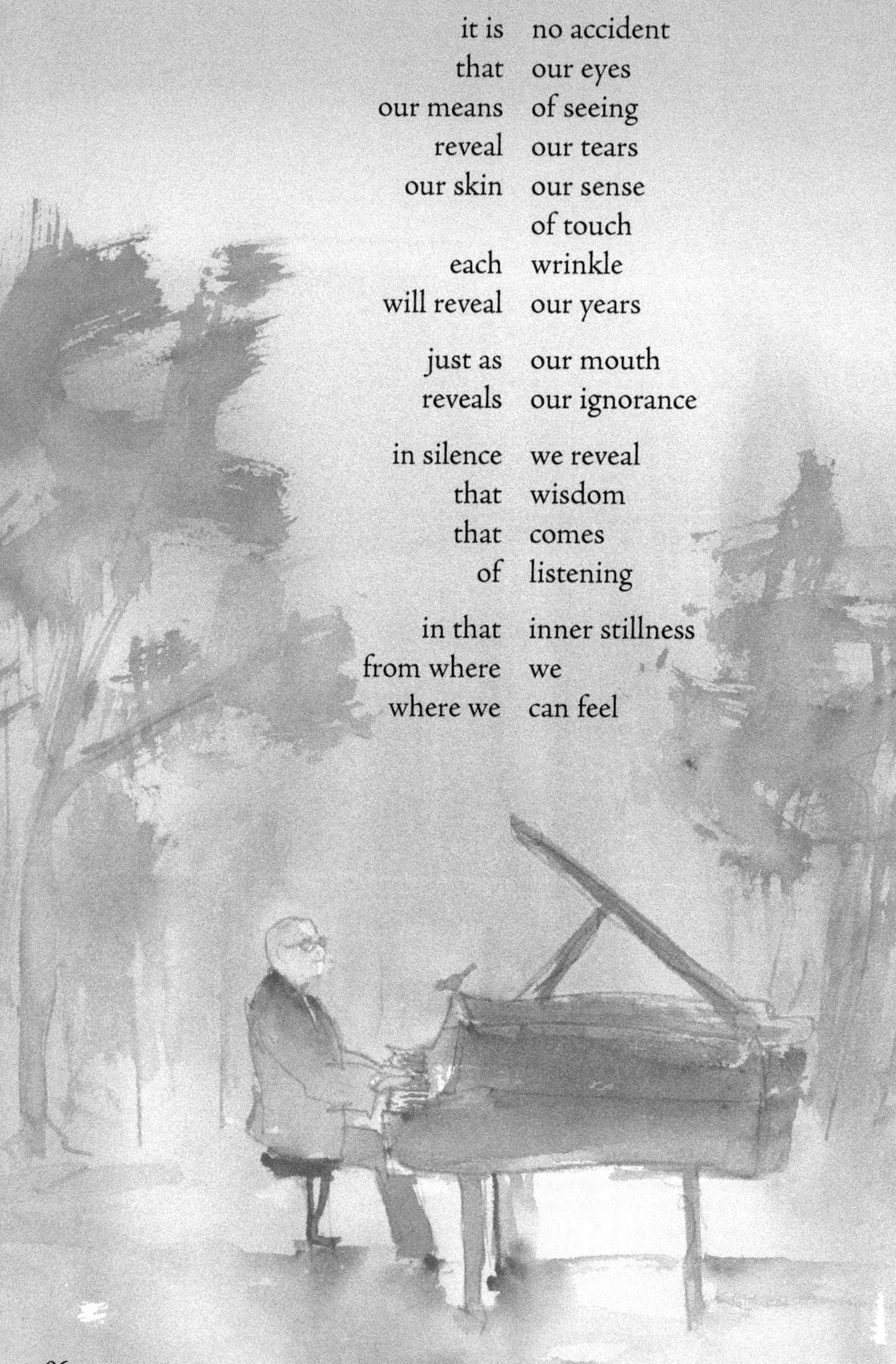

it is no accident
that our eyes
our means of seeing
reveal our tears
our skin our sense
of touch
each wrinkle
will reveal our years

just as our mouth
reveals our ignorance

in silence we reveal
that wisdom
that comes
of listening

in that inner stillness
from where we
where we can feel

listen
to   the silent
          ones

the silence that comes
in making   space
to hear   the noise
             of others

in jazz   they
know   this
you never play
every   note

on   silence
all songs sit

you leave spaces
bits   of silence
you let   things happen

a blankness   …
all potential is this
made   of nothing

you   now hold
white   pages
this pulp   of trees
and   cotton

that   suffers me
as I   suffer

this ink
just   to exist
it needed this

in this void   within
I feel   the universe
without

the emptiness   defines
all that is   without you

this sand

this dust
what has   become
of   us

what is   this destiny
to be   a grain
to just

be dust
the smallest   bit
of me

what is   this
that   this
that   makes me

this   bit
is this   my soul?
it   fell
into this   universe
of   all

and so   it flows

this me   a mystery
until   I meet
eternity

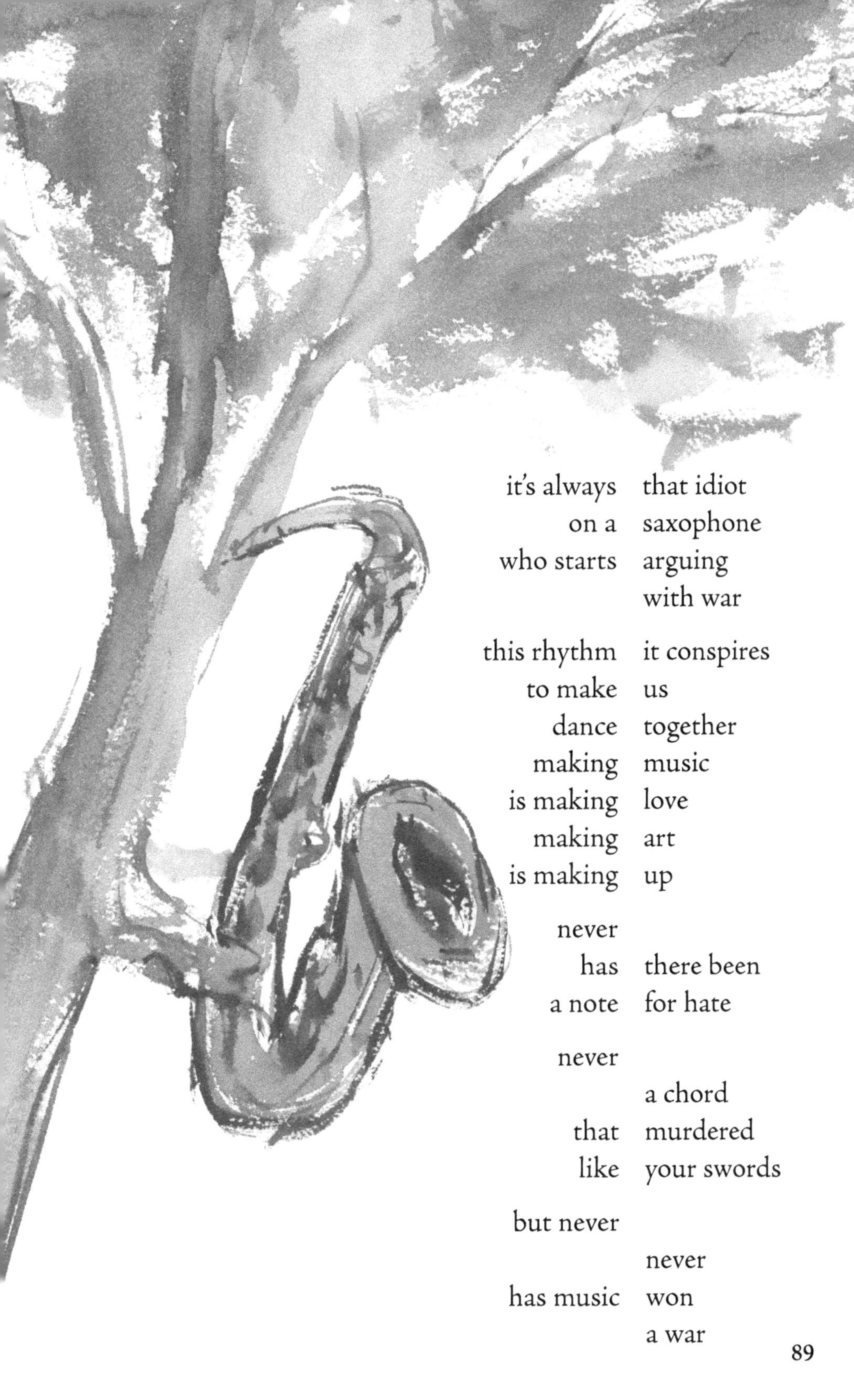

it's always that idiot
on a saxophone
who starts arguing
with war

this rhythm it conspires
to make us
dance together
making music
is making love
making art
is making up

never
has there been
a note for hate

never

a chord
that murdered
like your swords

but never

never
has music won
a war

wars are sold
the lie persists
you will win
they will die

music has no words
for this

it has no words

a song never
ends in peace

peace is what happens
while I sing
when I listen
while I dance

we come together
a momentary

pause

we forget to bicker
too busy listening
swaying
and holding
close

the crows   they know
they pick   our bones

the crows   they know
we believe   in war

more than   any song
more than   any poem

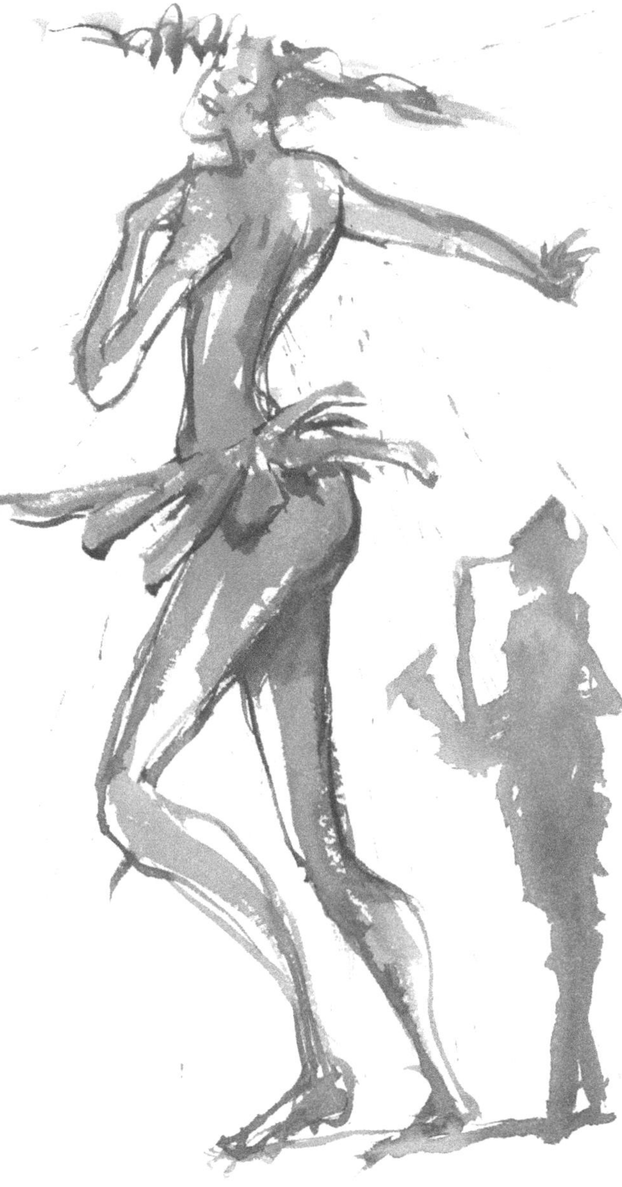

peace   is
the   happening
the   pause
that is   only caused
by idiots   on
their   saxophones
in their   tempting
tones

all art
its very   premise
is this

an   argument
with   war

only   in
that   stillness
when   we listen
when   we give
melody   meaning

only   then
can that   harmony
of we
be   truly
known

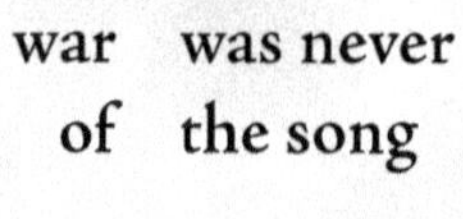

war   was never
of   the song
war is that silence
what   comes after

when   we
no longer sing

nothing to believe
we cannot dream

we enlist in enmity
this   we
now   enemies

to wage this war
we burn all love

we lose our soul
to burn the world

what are we then?

no longer brothers
just   soldiers
to one   another

when we fail
to sing together
ideals then falter

and doubt it gains power

utility it justifies
any means to
our end

as the worst get louder
that how grows darker

peace is defined
in that

how

by how I treat
another

by how I treat
the neighbor
and the stranger

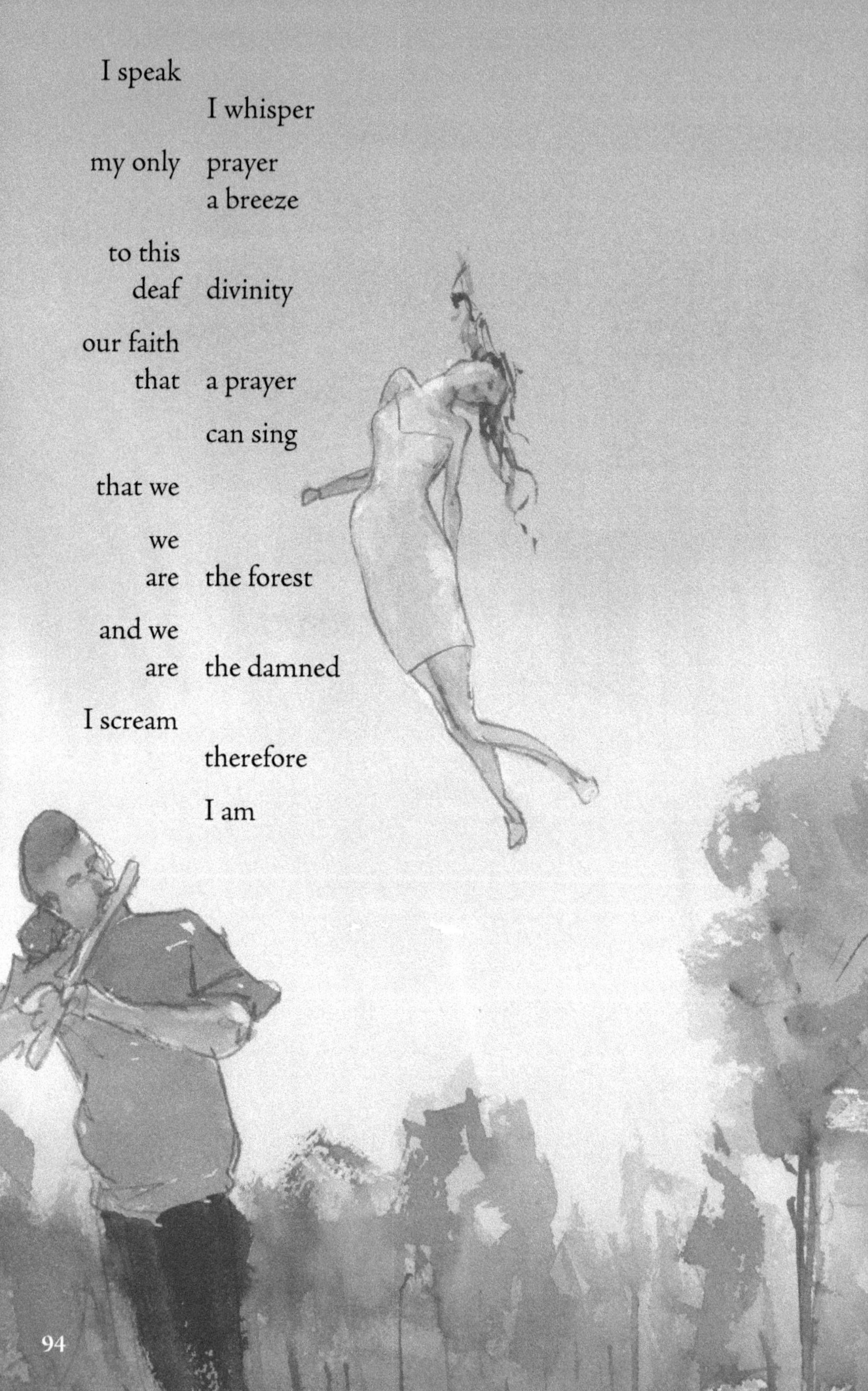

I speak
I whisper
my only prayer
a breeze
to this
deaf divinity
our faith
that a prayer
can sing
that we
we
are the forest
and we
are the damned
I scream
therefore
I am

god   is silent
only guns   I hear
our rage   I see

this faith   in bullets
never   each other

is this?
is this   the end?

are we   living now
at the end   of days?
at the end   of song?

prayers   they speak
to   revelations
is apocalypse   the new
salvation?

on this clock   of doom
are the seconds   coming?

have we   become
the beast?

I fear   not
the god   of love
but   you
the true   believer

the truth   we bury
is   each other

to believe
          that   revelations
          is now   salvation

our cynicism   is all

this question   rests
                 with god
when will   his optimism
                 fall?

man

                 is both
you   and me

we are

                 the belief
                 of god

we are

                 the clay
                 and dust
he breathed   into being us

all existence   rests
upon   this hope
that god   believe

god's faith   in us

                 is us

to lose   the faith
                 of god
will be   the fall
                 of man

only then
will this   world end

I am never   the disciple
I seek   dominion
I am   the roman
I am   the zealot
this cross   I wear
not the prince   of peace
but tool   of suffering
where   he hung
where   we
we sacrificed   his kindness

the illiterate   read
every word   literally

the more   I know
the less   I feel

to sharpen   this
the word   of god

to crucify   all enemies

I hold   this
this spear   of destiny
never   to prove
that   I believe

but that god
that   can bleed
belongs   this world
              to me

this   is my body
this   is my blood
my mind   it breaks

upon   the silence
of   the shepherd

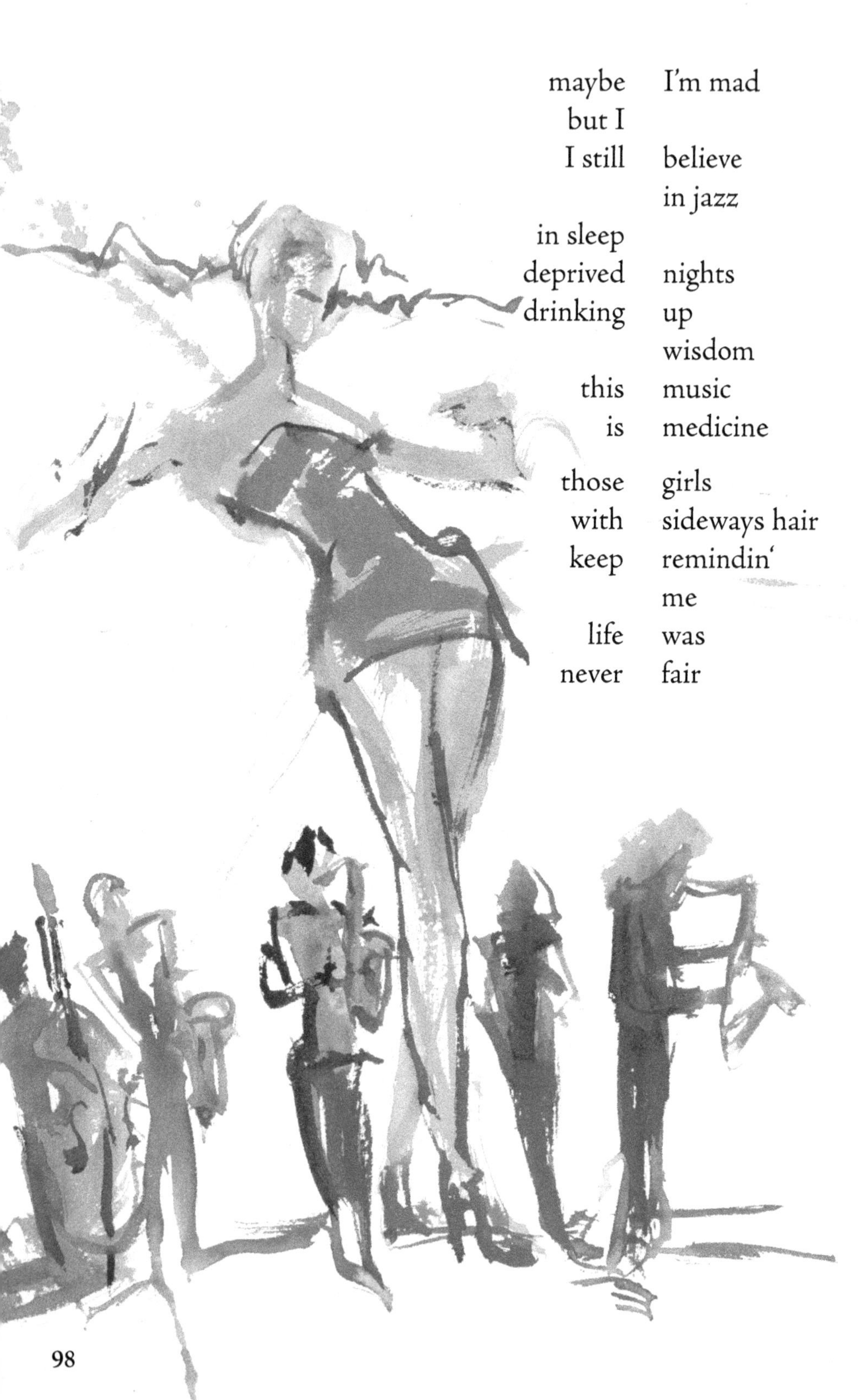

maybe   I'm mad
but I
I still   believe
         in jazz
in sleep
deprived   nights
drinking   up
         wisdom
this   music
is   medicine
those   girls
with   sideways hair
keep   remindin'
         me
life   was
never   fair

each   prayer
just   desire
never   answered
each   wish
paid   in blood
at the   expense
of what   we love

helen   her beauty
set   the world
            to war
while   cassandra
that   witch
we   ignored
her   curse
of   prediction
was   our doom
all   she said
it   came true

her   worry
was god's   warning
her   prophecy
no man   believed

*"in our war   for love
we murder
all   we love"*

the music   I obey
in hearing   I believe
in listening   how I feel
arguing   with notes
pleading   with melody
I seek   my muse
hearing her   thru history

this beat   I believe
trippin'   over prophecy
nothing   is free
not even   trouble
when jazz   is all you love

I'm not   agnostic
I'm not   waitin' to see
I've got   the rhythm of god
sittin' right in front of me

each heart   beat bleeds
upon   these strings
busy fingers   that dream
jazz   into bein'
despite   all
our   disbelievin'

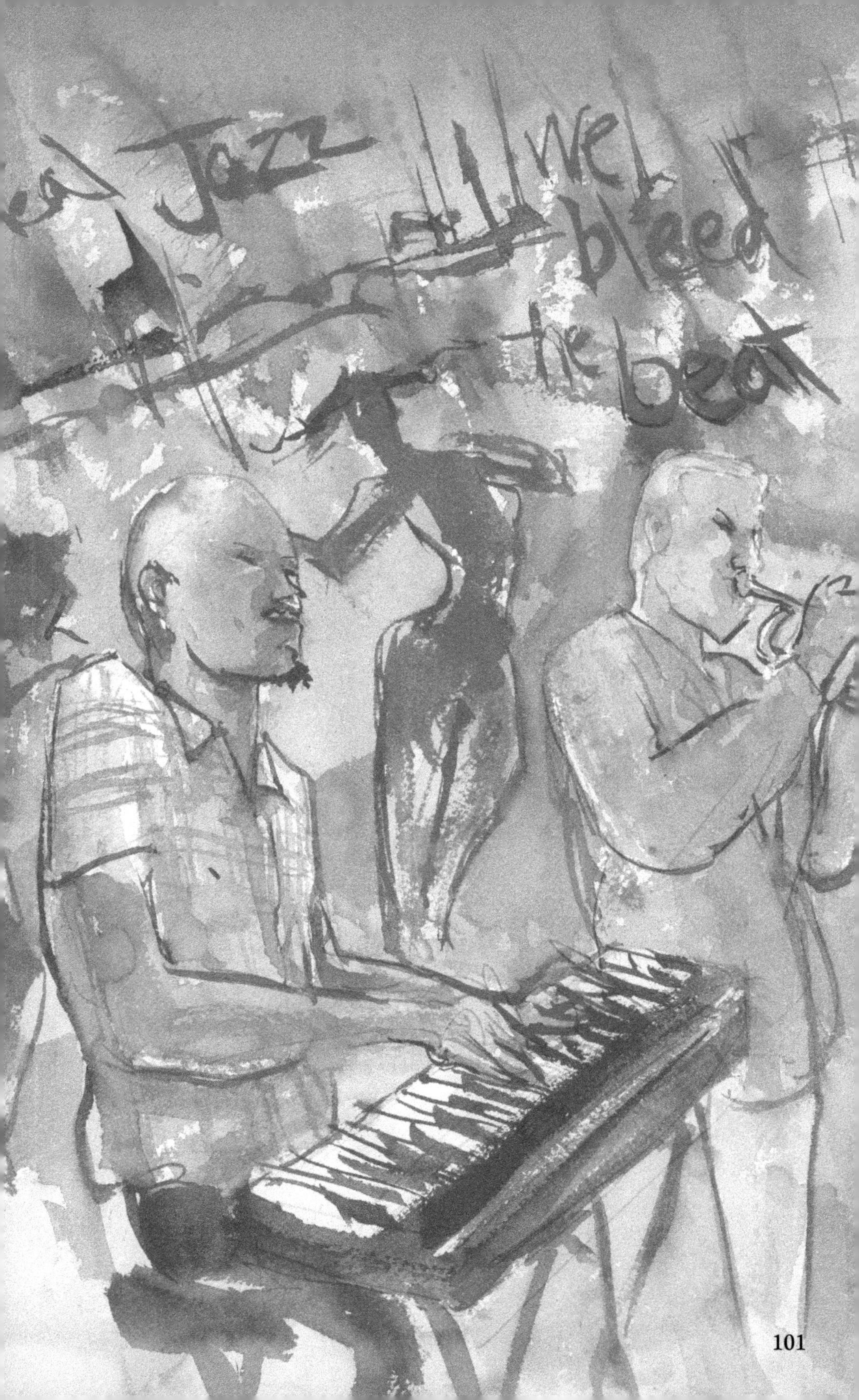
Jazz
we
bleed
the beat

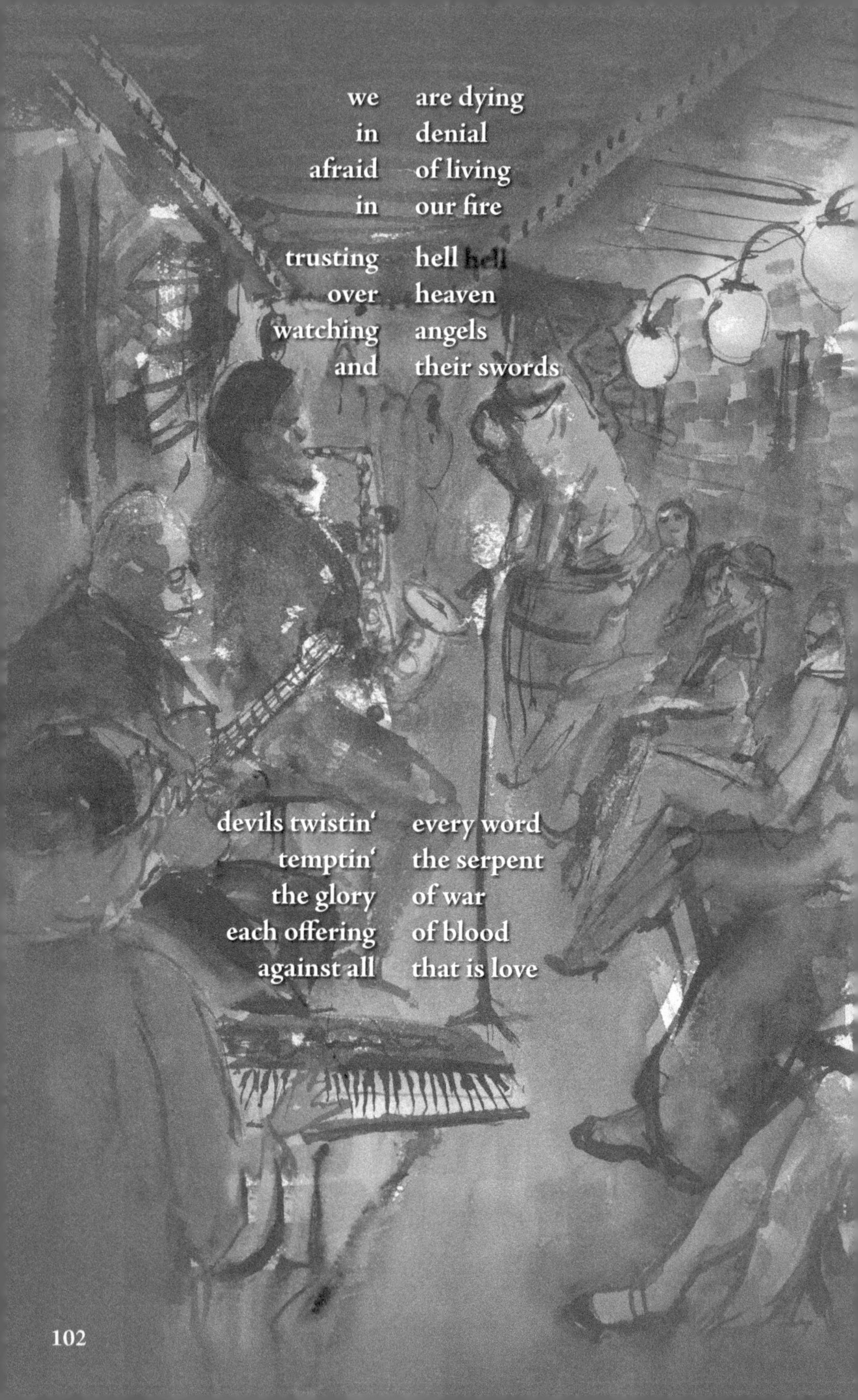

we   are dying
in   denial
afraid   of living
in   our fire

trusting   hell
over   heaven
watching   angels
and   their swords

devils twistin'   every word
temptin'   the serpent
the glory   of war
each offering   of blood
against all   that is love

the serpent   was obeyed
our return   forbidden
failed servants   of eden
banished long   before history

in that   garden
where god   set us free
to wield   the sword
                   of paradise

we burn   the tree
                   of life
but   its roots
still rise   within us

its roots   are us
by   its seed
that apple   remains
evoking   provoking us

death is reborn   thru each
and every   one of us
blaming   only eve
never   our masculine
but adam   did listen
both acts   forbidden
we fell   between
heaven   and hell

of cain and abel   we descend
a brother   damned
the curse   to live
never   to be
our brothers   keeper

as the favorite   of god
bled upon   that sand
the   rhythm
of   our wrong
we   will never
                     understand

in the end   all our stuff
our destiny   is dust
the real answer   is us
all   our stories
will be   history
forgotten fossils   of memory
it is   our song
that will   live on
maybe   I'm mad
but   this god
who   made me
is   makin' me
believe   in jazz

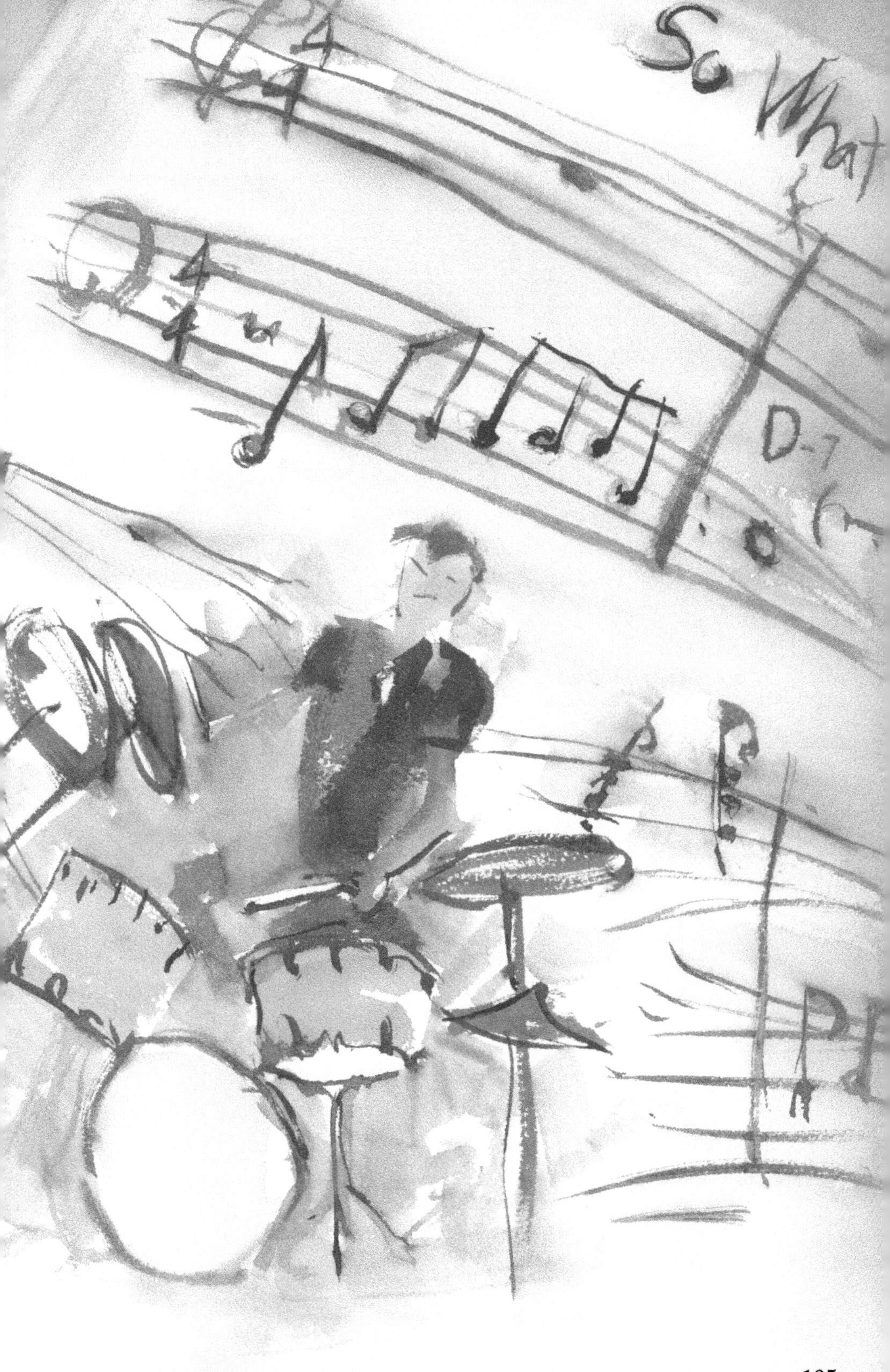
So What
D-7

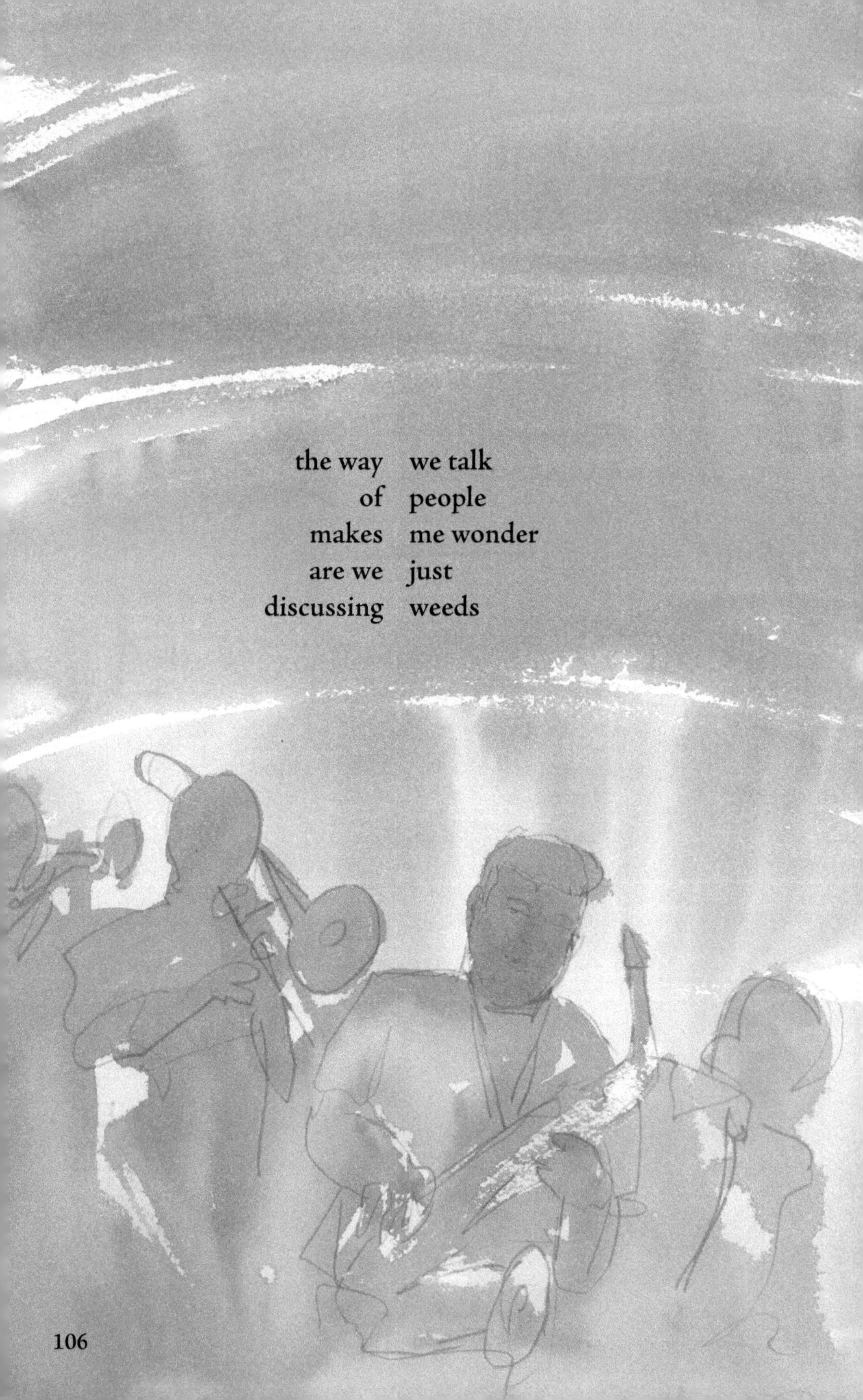
the way   we talk
       of   people
   makes   me wonder
   are we   just
discussing   weeds

weed
the people
a more perfect
union

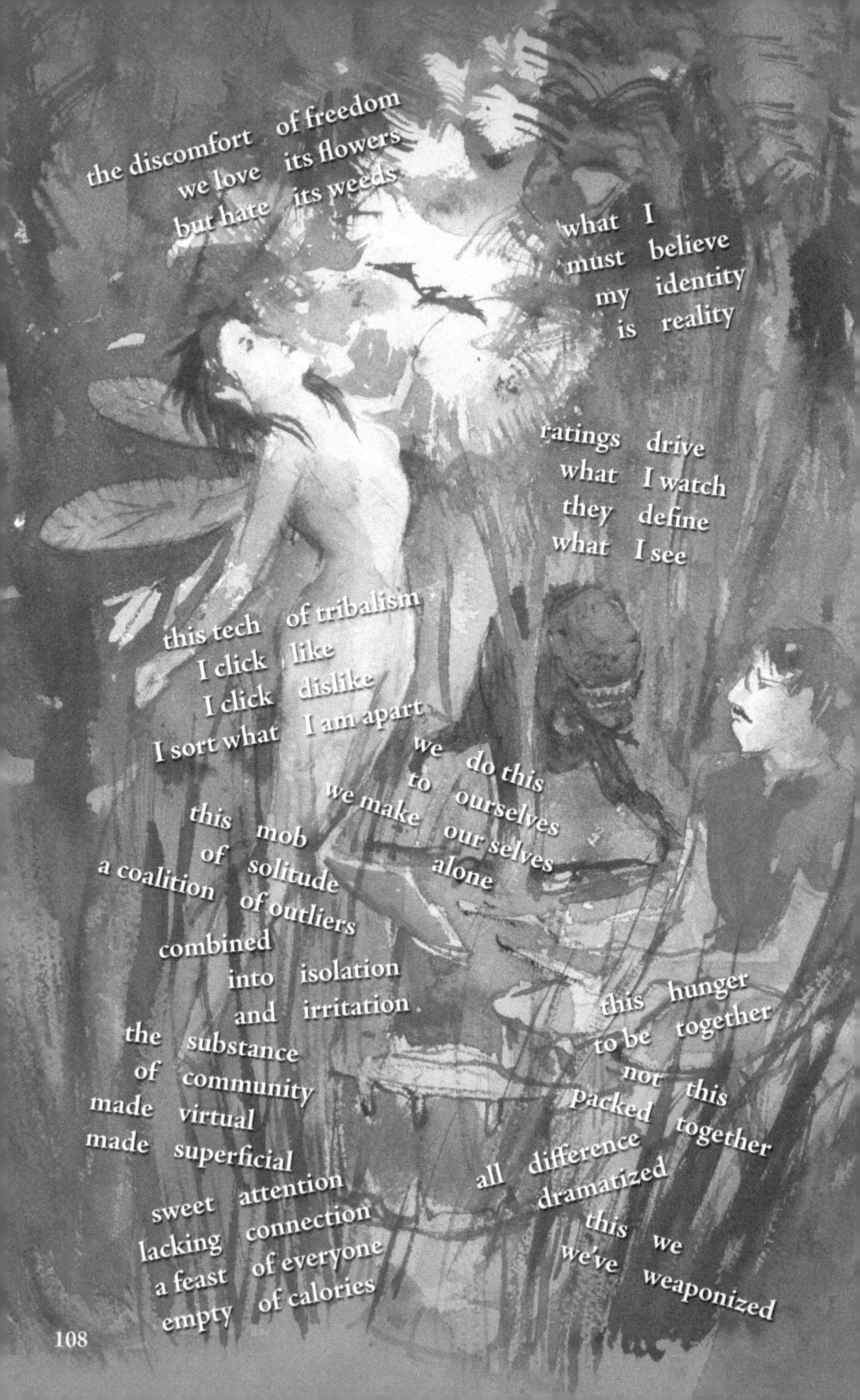

the discomfort   of freedom
we love   its flowers
but hate   its weeds

what   I
must   believe
my   identity
is   reality

ratings   drive
what   I watch
they   define
what   I see

this tech   of tribalism
I click   like
I click   dislike
I sort what   I am apart

we   do this
to   ourselves
we make   our selves
alone

this   mob
of   solitude
a coalition   of outliers
combined
into   isolation
and   irritation
the   substance
of   community
made   virtual
made   superficial
sweet   attention
lacking   connection
a feast   of everyone
empty   of calories

this   hunger
to be   together
not   this
packed   together
all   difference   dramatized
this   we
we've   weaponized

these groups   made for me
are the bubbles   dividing us
by algorithm   controlled
this assault   spreading salt
all that   grounds
all sense   of real
now   lost

dissent   is watered
in   isolation
this me   this group

all my   identity
feeds into   this need
to be rid   of you

just as   love
is watered   in together
it erodes   this me
into   us

a richer   wider sense
not identity   but community
not just me   but we

in meeting   strangers
in making   others
into   brothers
this we   will grow

this we   grows wild
out of   control

like   weeds
this   we
the flowers   we
refuse   to meet

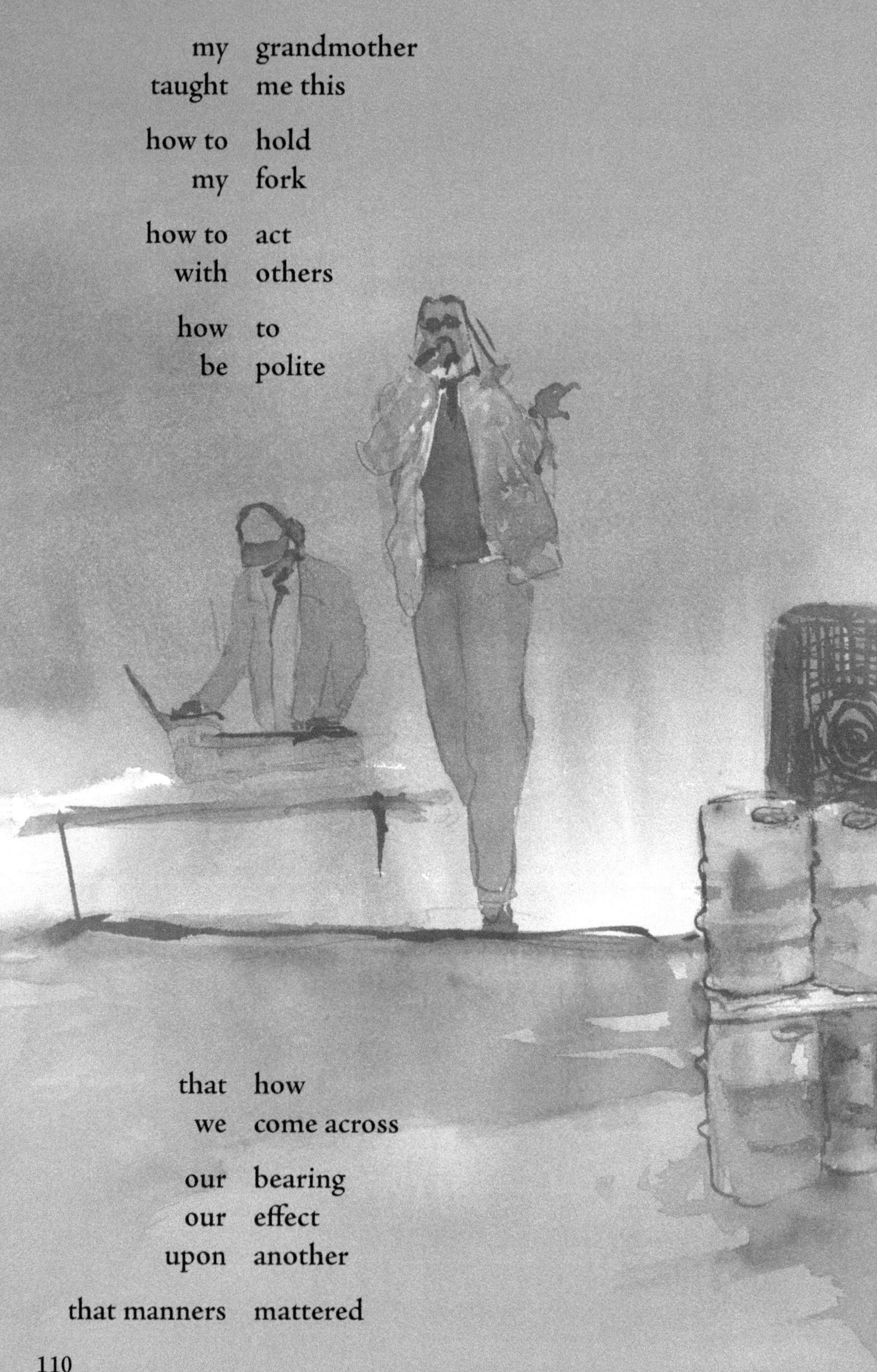

my   grandmother
taught me this
how to hold
my   fork

how to act
with   others

how   to
be   polite

that   how
we   come across
our   bearing
our   effect
upon   another

that manners   mattered

110

in basic   my drill
taught me   my right
from   my left
to stand   at attention
attention   to detail
those   push ups
hardened   me

my military   bearing
my visible   manner
this is   discipline
this is   being a soldier
we wore   boots
never   sneakers

I said   sir or ma'am
and never   swore
visibly   in uniform
even as   I learned to curse
in every   language

manners   mattered then

etiquette   was once
the visage   of being
              conservative

this myth   of plantations
still   wears
a polite   veneer

the southern gentleman
is now   gone
with   the wind

111

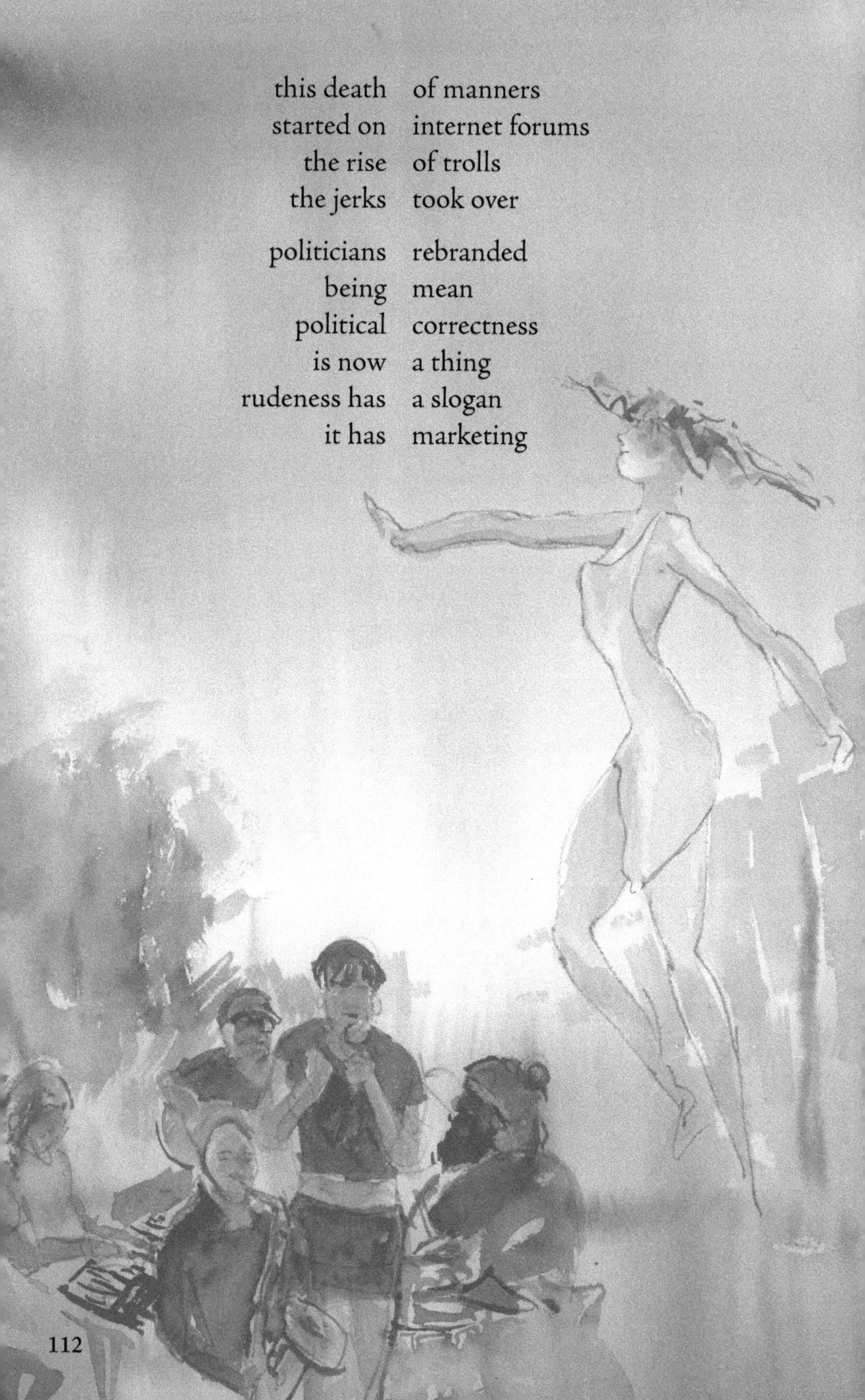

this death of manners
started on internet forums
the rise of trolls
the jerks took over

politicians rebranded
being mean
political correctness
is now a thing
rudeness has a slogan
it has marketing

in just   saying
any damn   fool thing
whatever comes   to mind
no matter   how absurd
no matter   how
we affect   one another

this   insistence
that   we
have   a right
to be   rude

as   a child
we never   disputed
this   was
being   stupid

without   manners
how can   you and me?
how can   this we?
how can   we?
peacefully   disagree?

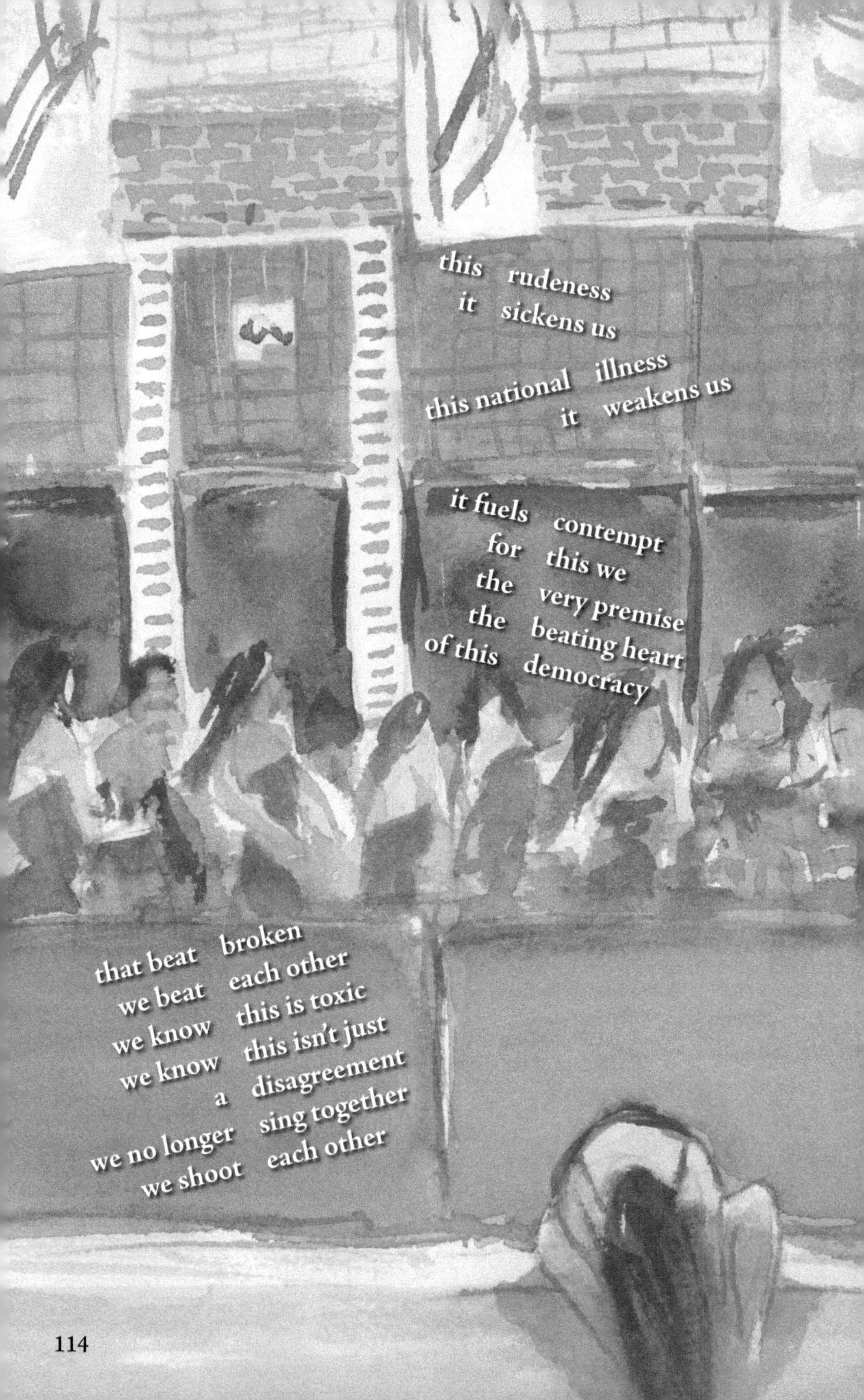

this   rudeness
it   sickens us

this national   illness
it   weakens us

it fuels   contempt
for   this we
the   very premise
the   beating heart
of this   democracy

that beat   broken
we beat   each other
we know   this is toxic
we know   this isn't just
a   disagreement
we no longer   sing together
we shoot   each other

114

this raw   contempt
echoes   our society
our failed   marriages
our lack   of faith
this rise   of none
and love   of conspiracy

this decline   in manners
is   the herald
and root   cause
the rot   behind
this nation's   decline

all   the while
the jerks   and trolls
now arguing   for supremacy
insist   that this
this lack   of kindness
this rudeness   proves
that being   mean
is what   being strong
now   means

the magic   of fire
begins   my dance
I obey   its blaze
in belief   I burn
casting these   my shadow flees
my belief   is giving birth

each night   I find in flames
it rules   my imagination
will the dawn   ever
come   again?

can I   doubt the dark?
when I am   its child

I fall   for the easy
for lords   repeating
comfort   to my ears
all I want   to hear
to burn   the system down

for kings prey   upon the crowd
they sing   of kingdoms
that might   is the cure
to every   weakness
if I let them   lead us

as kindling   is
to fire

I kneel   obedient
in fear

but in   that coronation
I meet   their domination
that throne   of fire
will be   my pyre
freedom   ever sold
for the gold   of crowns

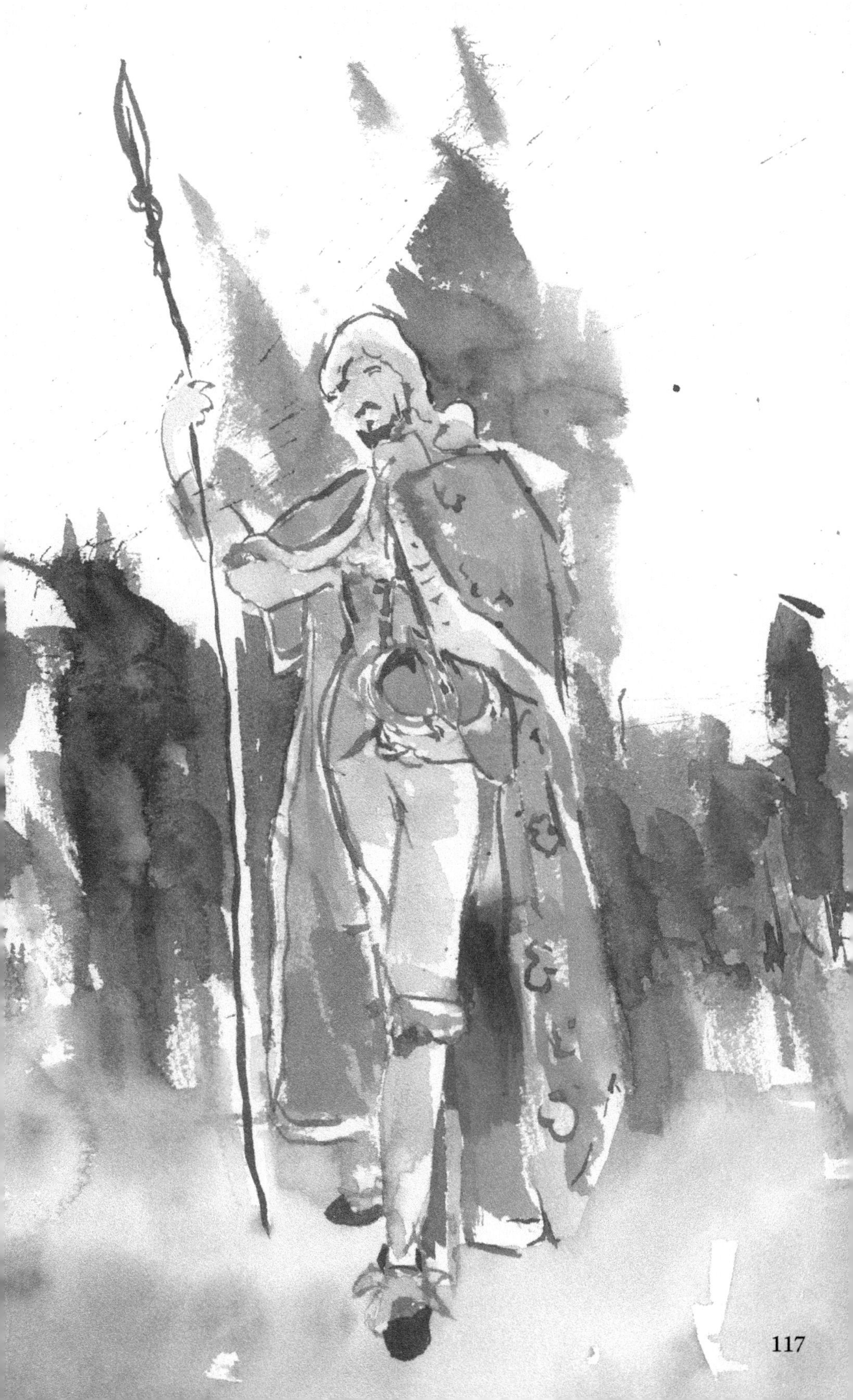

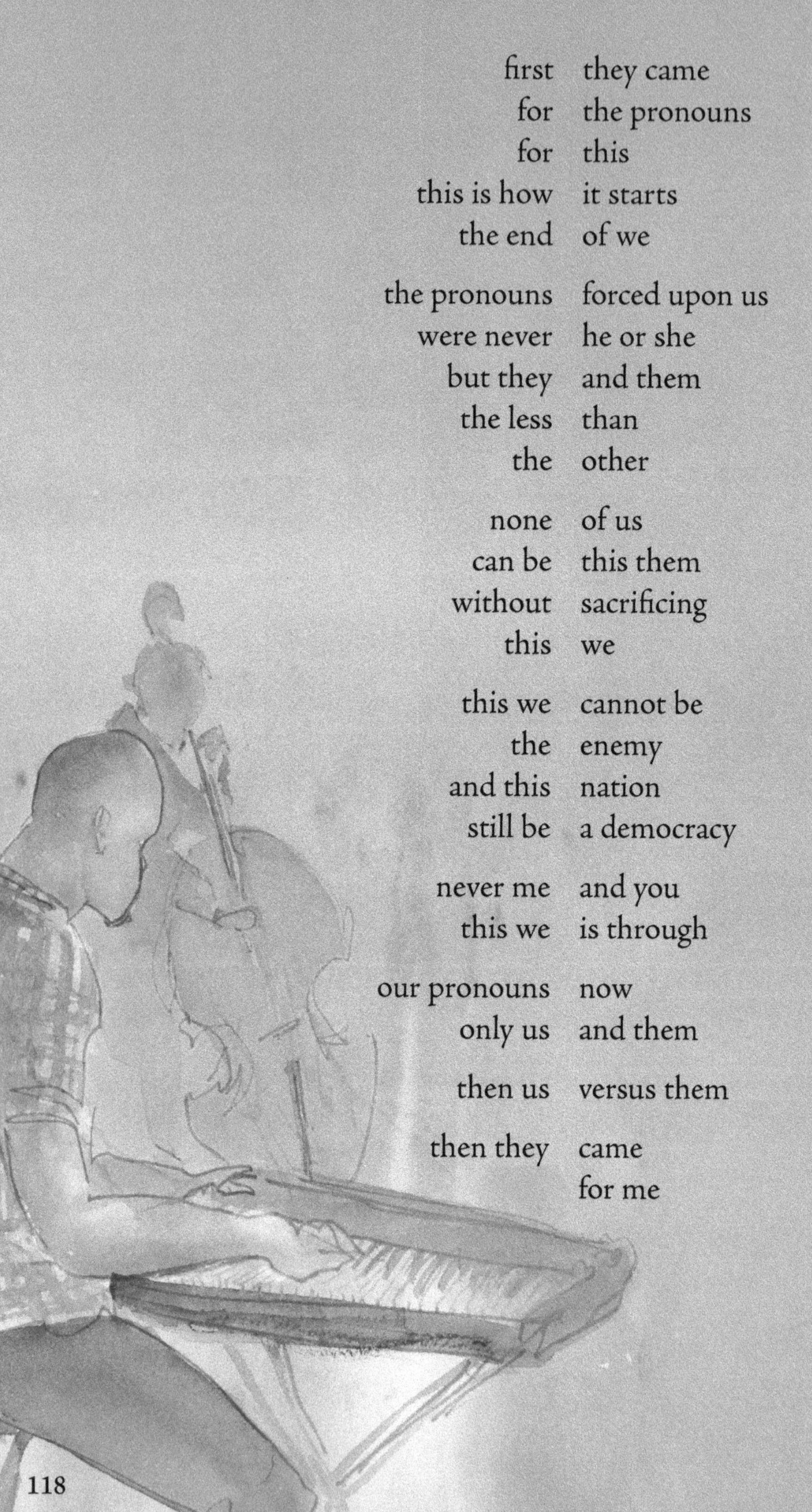

first   they came
for   the pronouns
for   this
this is how it starts
the end   of we

the pronouns forced upon us
were never   he or she
but they   and them
the less   than
the   other

none   of us
can be   this them
without   sacrificing
this   we

this we   cannot be
the   enemy
and this   nation
still be   a democracy

never me   and you
this we   is through

our pronouns now
only us   and them

then us   versus them

then they   came
            for me

will I   ever know
what   the flowers
call   themselves

are flowers   he or she
        or they?
are these just   turns of phrase

what gender   can flowers be
we teach   children
the birds   and the bees
what does that   really mean?
what kinky   things
do flowers   do with bees

his stamina   of pollen
her stigma   of pistil
seems like   flowers
have both   of these

we don't   call them
he or she   or they
just flowers   just roses

but I   will never know
the names   that flowers
call   themselves

if you knew   that roses
hated being   called roses

would   you cede
to the   flowers
our   power
to   decide

what   they call
and how   they see
        themselves

the hardiness   I find
    in little   things
  a vitality   that
 overwhelms   the trees

  they climb   they strangle
    as life   goes wild
   a garden   choking
      upon   its weeds

never subject   to
      our   law
  obedient   only
   to god   and nature

            a garden   now
             ruled   by weeds
                    by we

          isn't this   what
          freedom   means?

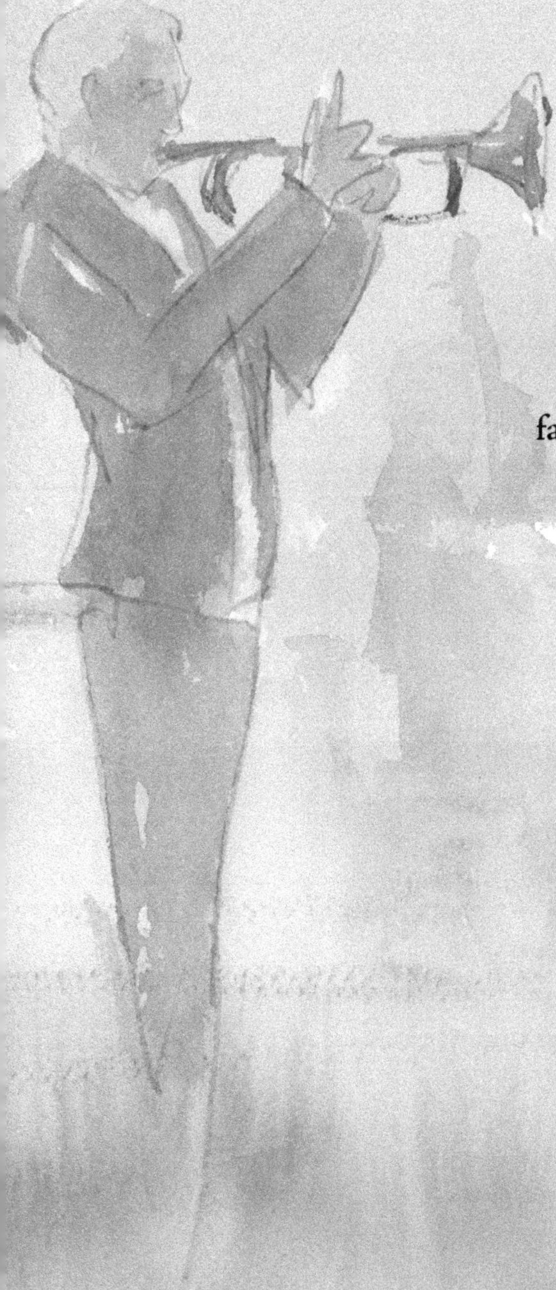

the weeds
are what we call
the flowers we
never wanted

the garden
in its order
in its ordered
rows
is not the garden
that nature grows

the lawless weeds
obey only the birds
they suffer the winds
directions
falling where they will

nature knows
no lines
no borders
soil is soil
seeds are seeds

those born weeds
will rile the rule of roses
while I
I love the wildness
found in nameless
flowers

I love that
nature finds
its perfection
in rampant imperfection

the gardener   rules
by spade   by hoe
a dictator   deciding
who stays   who goes

there can   only be
just me   my kind
without   kindness
only   the good
we   defined

without   conflict
without   difference
a garden   of
singular   identity

without   wildness
without   weird
you weeded   out roughness
that grit   was resilience
your flowers now   falling prey
to disease   and predator

nietzsche's   maxim
what does not   kill it
has never   made
a sameness   stronger
natural   selection
is driven   by difference

the noise   we silence
the heartbeat   of innovation
how this   democracy
    breathes

for freedom   speaks
in   gardens
overrun   by weeds

you sing of flowers
but hate against
          the weeds?

they sprout unbidden
             unwanted
intruding   upon
your ordered rows

maybe this isn't so

what you   call weeds
another will call flowers

strangers only until
you've   met them
and learn   their names

introduce yourself
show   these weeds
           hospitality

start   a conversation
stir up questions

can a petal be subversive?

can a bloom be nefarious?

can being born
a flower   be illegal?

can we love
        the weeds?

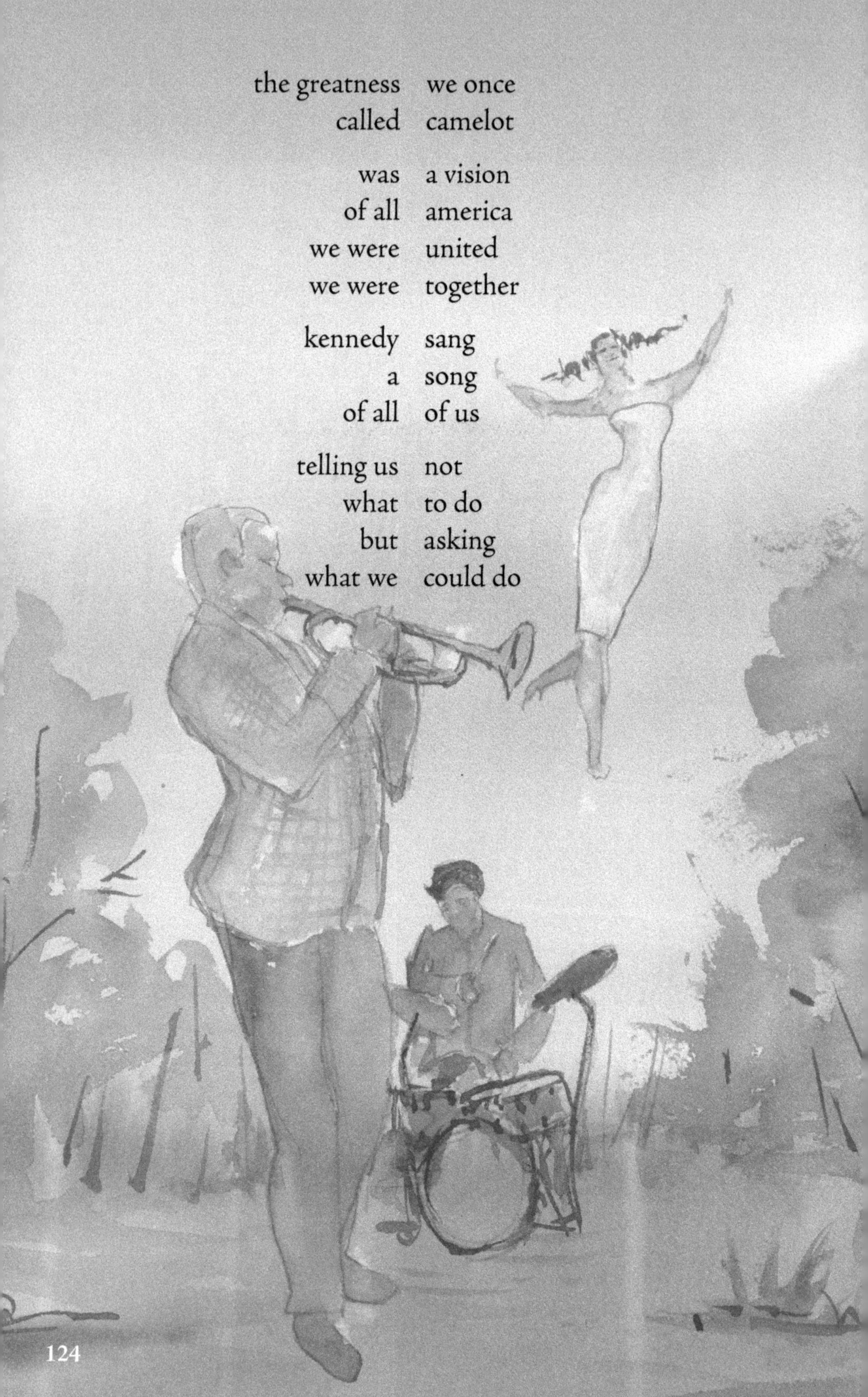
the greatness   we once
called   camelot

was   a vision
of all   america
we were   united
we were   together

kennedy   sang
a   song
of all   of us

telling us   not
what   to do
but   asking
what we   could do

124

this was   not
a song   of us
versus   them

but   a song
that   saw
that this   america
is all   of us

this   dream
of   brotherhood
across   diversity

and yet   this dream
has not   awoken

it never was   a reality

just   a possibility

they shot   the singer

they shot   kennedy

and they   shot his brother

they shot   martin luther king

and   lennon too

they are   still shooting

they are   shooters
who shoot   the singers
they shoot   the dreamers

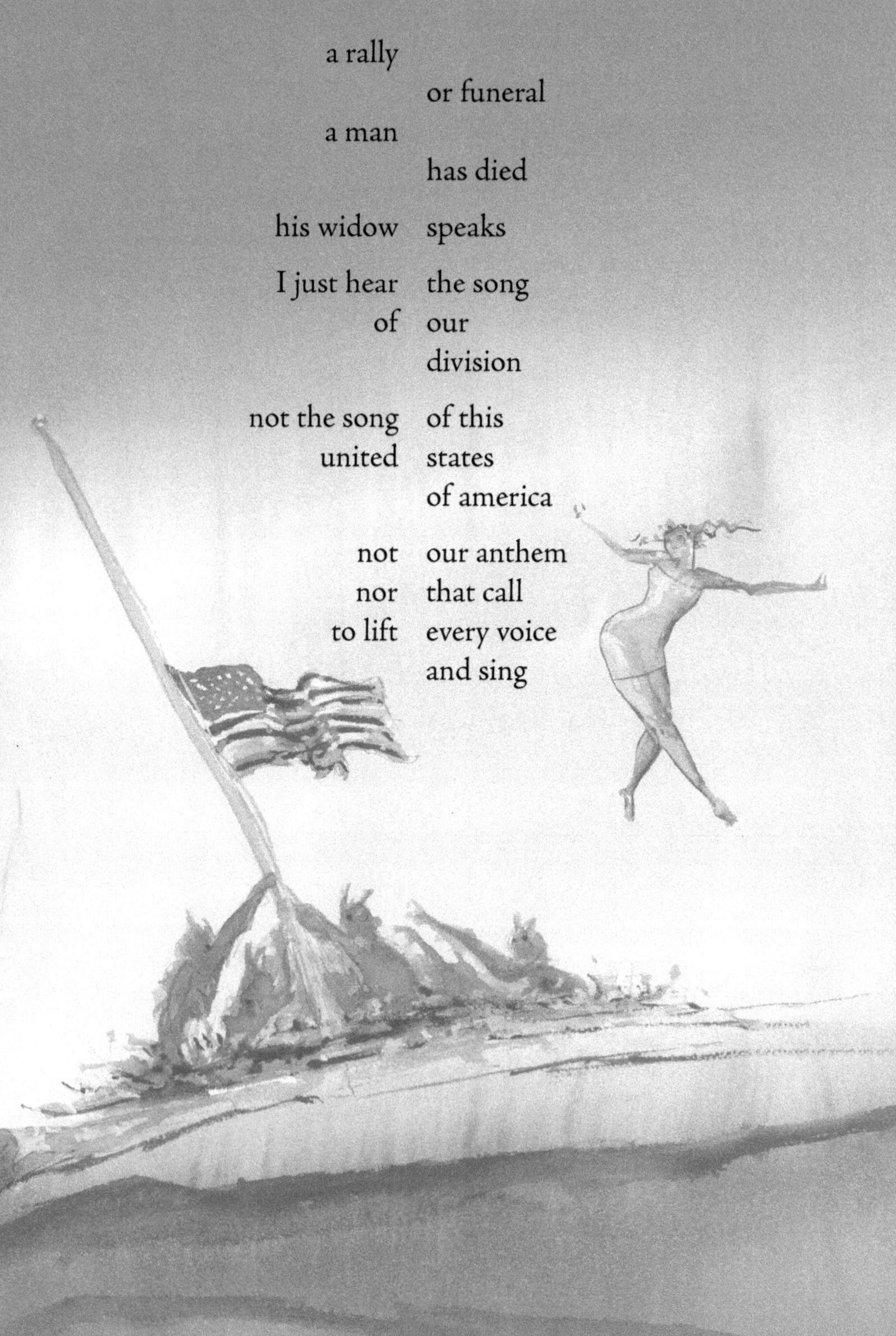

a rally
or funeral
a man
has died
his widow speaks
I just hear the song
of our
division
not the song of this
united states
of america
not our anthem
nor that call
to lift every voice
and sing

but an   america
  of us   and them

  of us   versus them

not to   mourn
  his   needless death

but that   we
  we   must
adopt   his cause

if you   are not
            for him
for every   thing
  he   stood for
  you   must be
            the enemy

you are   either
            with us
or you   are one
            of them

our flag   flies
on flag   poles
at half   staff
in honor   in mourning
of one   who should
never   have died

while
we   the people
we fly   our flag
upside   down
we cry   we mourn
that this   is now
this is when   this democracy

this democracy   has died

I hear   this
national   anthem
my hand   over my heart
then my hand by my eye
            saluting

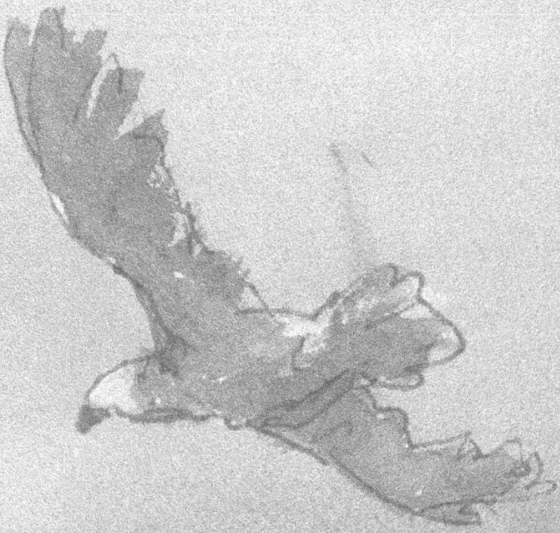

does that   star
spangled   banner
still   wave
over   the land
of   the free
the   home
of   the brave

is this   song I hear
from   a funeral
for a   fallen man

or   is this
the   funeral
for   america

the song   of us
versus   them

is the song   of
every   nation
every   religion

your song   of god
is   never
the song   of
heaven   above

only when
the thousand   thousand creatures
are free
to sing   their song
no matter   how wrong

only   then
will   justice
ring

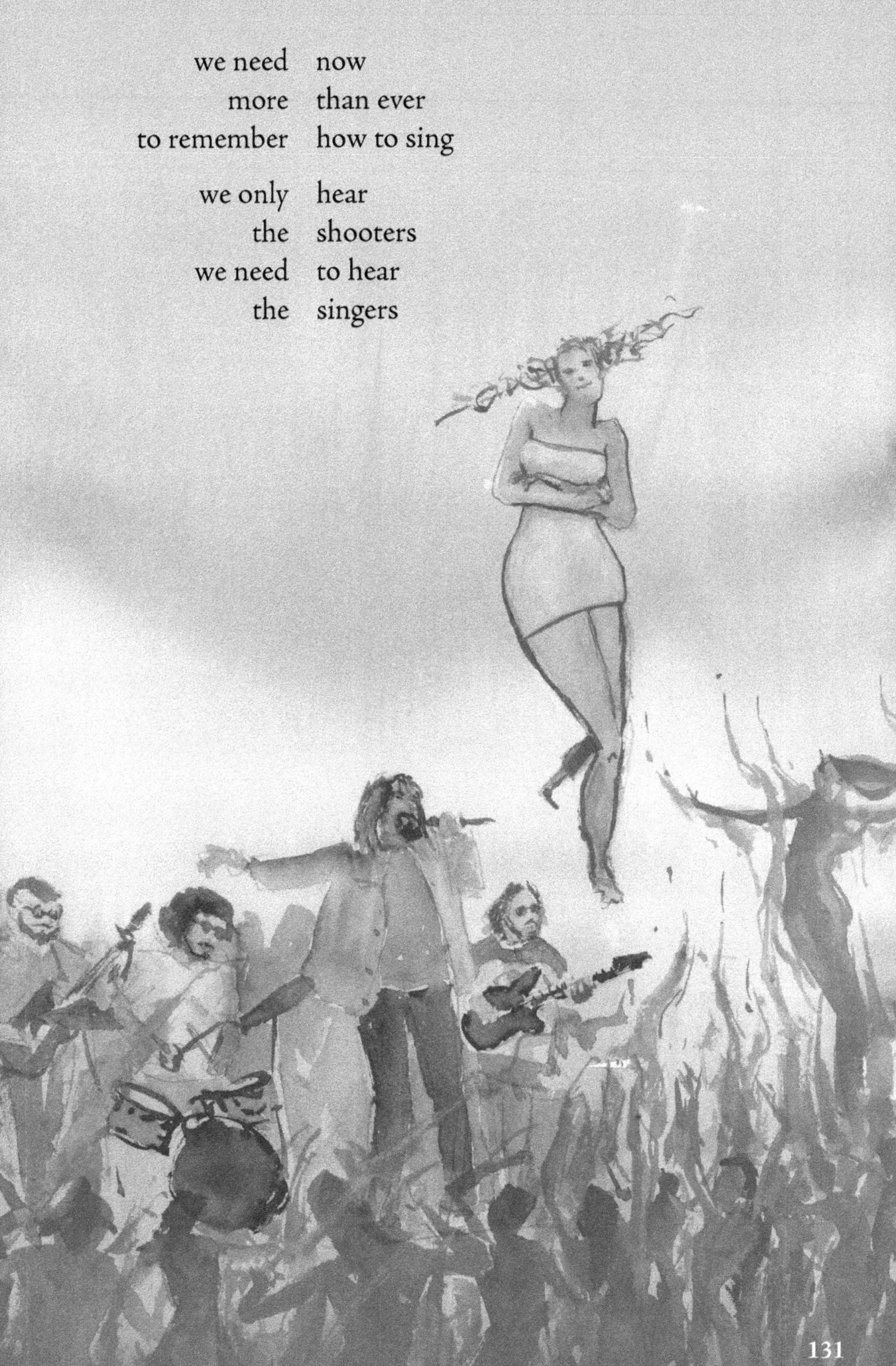

we need   now
more   than ever
to remember   how to sing

we only   hear
the   shooters
we need   to hear
the   singers

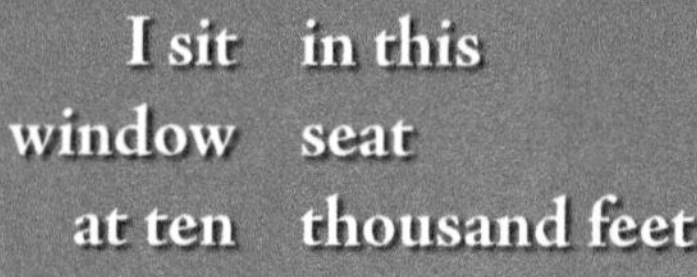

I sit   in this
window   seat
at ten   thousand feet

I see   america
not united   nor divided
but looking   down
and out   this window
at the earth   below
this land   this dirt
this country   between
two shining   seas

and   I hear
the   song
of   america

the song
of america

at ten thousand feet

I look   next to me
and   see
travelers   just like me
with a place to be
some place   to see
going home   or moving
leaving   for new jobs
or returning   for lost love

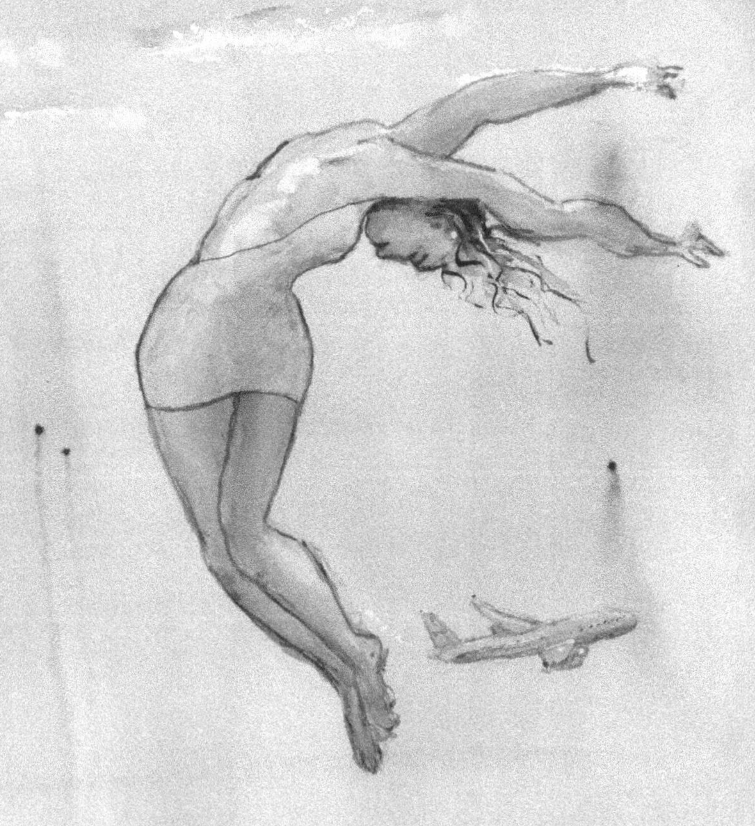

when   flying
through   the sky
we forget our politics
we cannot see party

we buckle up together
this is   the real
           america

this   is freedom
this   is all of us
just doing our thing
it's speaking and traveling
just looking for somewhere

always trying to be better
what   matters
is getting there

most   of us
never   looking
out these   windows

we sleep   to dream
only looking   at
these   screens

I hear   the song
of   babies
seeking   mothers

the scream   of need

behind   me
an eruption   of arguing
a stewardess   bumped
     into   him

that final   straw
we project   upon it
all life's   frustration
triggering   reactions
of broken   proportion

this is   life
out of   balance

a grown   man
who   had enough

we never   outgrow
that scream   of need

this is   what
is   wrong
with most   of us

we've   had
too   much

we are   dozing
stuck here   cramped
seat backs   pushed
against   my knees

I need   space
too close   for comfort
I can't   stand
nor   get away

who   ever said
that plane   seats
should   be beds?

never   designed
for   rest
but for   packing
people
against   each
other

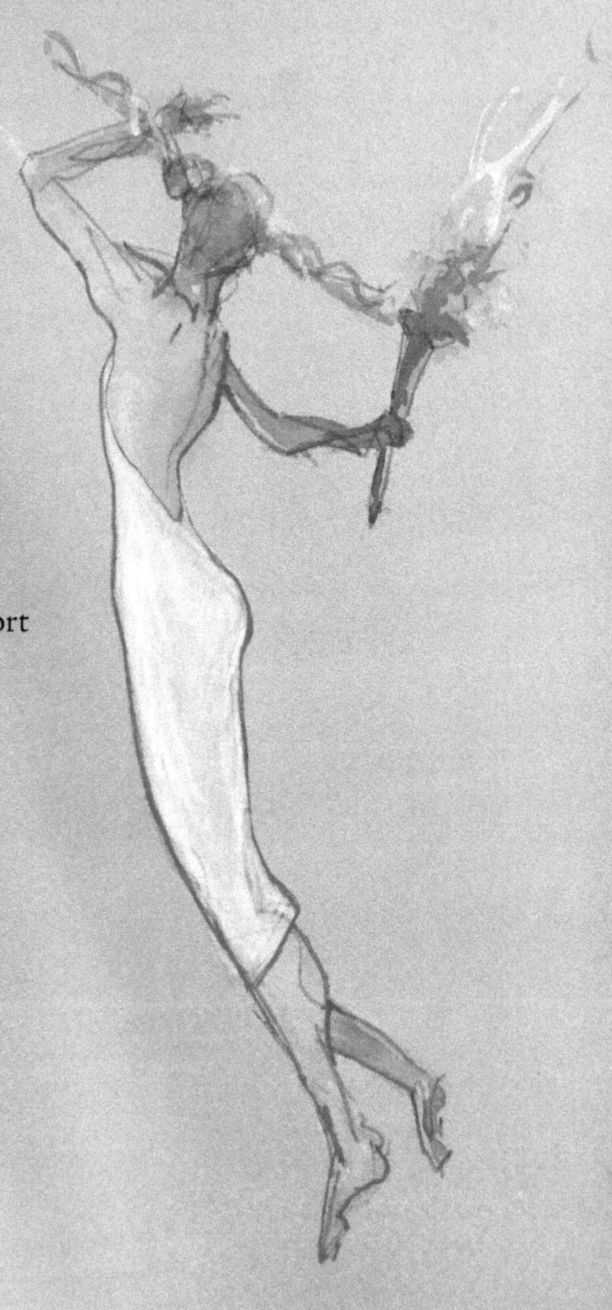

this   contempt
this   rage
is less   about
each   other

but about   ourselves

we are   stuck

this world   in which
we find   ourselves
was not   made
for   us

we need   profit
more than   people

we conflate   injustice
with our   discomfort
all   of us
are just   too close

we blame   each other

this   world
we designed   it
we packed   it
against   us

we are   inside
never   outside
never in   the world
that was   made
for   us

we are   the exiles
the weeds   forbidden
what god   pulled
from   the garden

in traveling   we see
each   other

others   we
never   know

we see   instead
the shared   struggle

we see   in them
our   struggle

in flight   empathy
is forced   upon us

just traveling   we assume
those next   to us

those packed   against us

are still   people
just   like us

we become   them

the foreigner   the migrant farmer
the immigrant   the stranger

those without   a home
or place   to be

all   we own
luggage   and
a   plane seat

we see   others
without   the othering
as real people   in their lives
the love   of family
the mourning   of loss
in partings   and reunions
in business   and vacation

all   so different
and   yet
all   stuck together
all   heading somewhere

as my   plane
flees   the sun
I hear   the song
of america

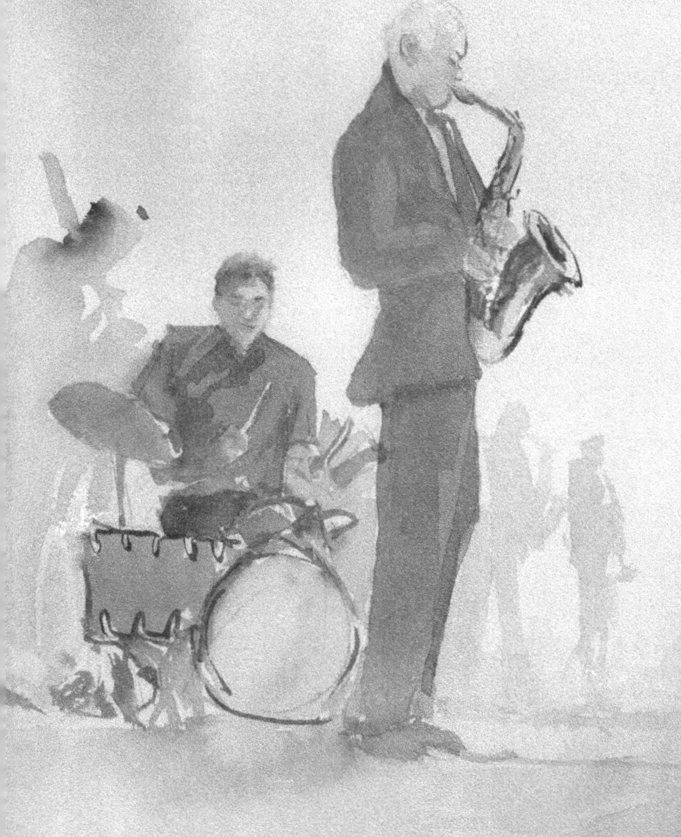

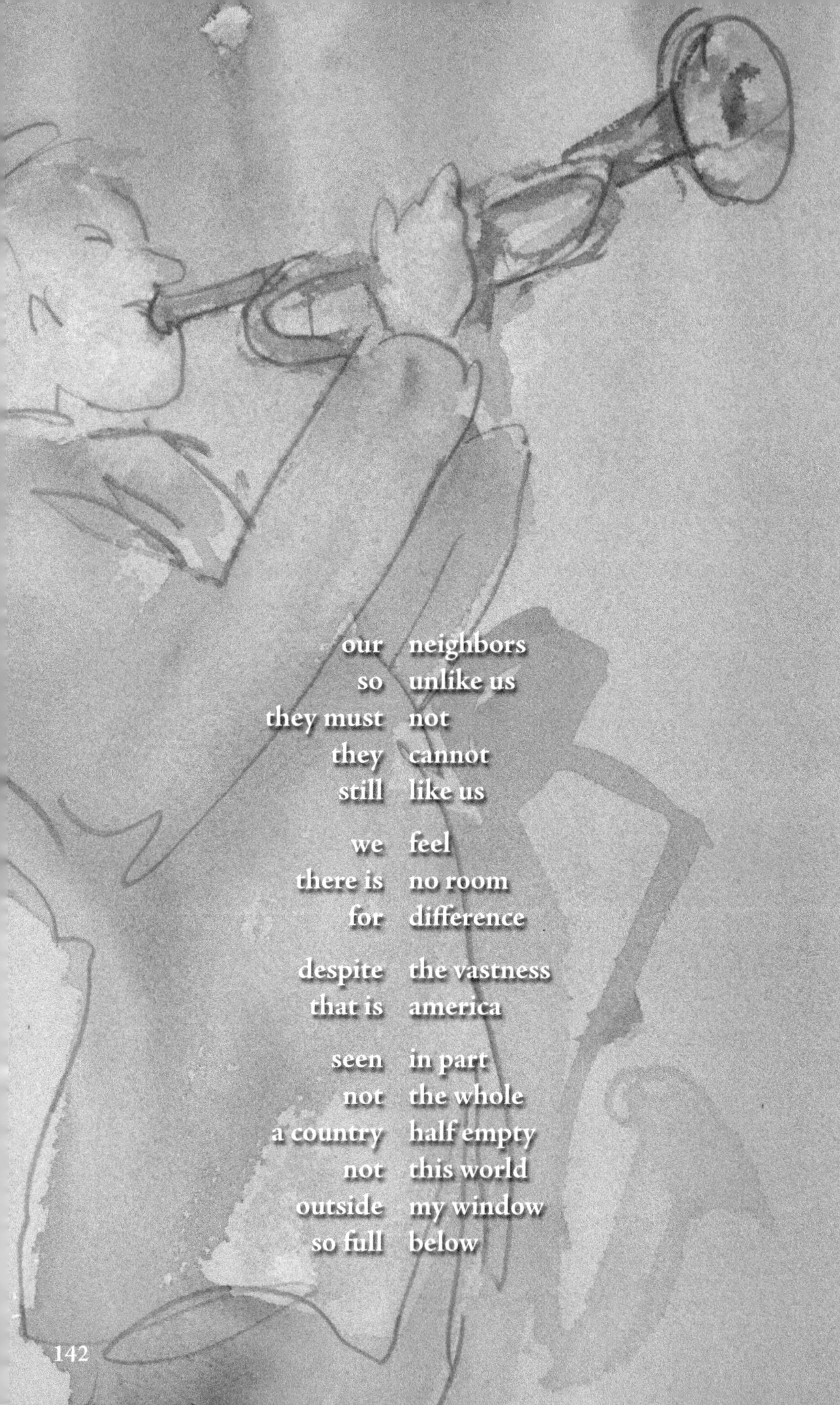

our neighbors
so unlike us
they must not
they cannot
still like us

we feel
there is no room
for difference

despite the vastness
that is america

seen in part
not the whole
a country half empty
not this world
outside my window
so full below

142

I see   from
my window   seat
the   grapevine

a thousand   thousand trucks
crawling   up and down
this mountain pass
every day   and by
              the hour

the blood   stream
of head   lights
that   reaches
across   america

across these interstates
that   connect us

our   prosperity
our   commerce
our   nation's
beating   heart

all this   activity
all these   cars
              and trucks

this

              is us

we trust this pilot
with our lives
regardless of
his views

just as he
must trust
his instruments

the advice of
air traffic control
and those safety experts

the magic of flight
that we trust
the seatbelt light

stewardesses stand above us
arms dance in pantomime
exits oxygen
help yourself
before you help
each other

the pilots and industry
in checklists and procedures
all making sure we get
where we are going

by mechanics by ground crew
by security screening
every bag

preparing for anything
this community
that makes us feel
flying is safe

we can leave
the sun behind
and let the night
hold sway

we can fly even blind
only because we believe
in this technology

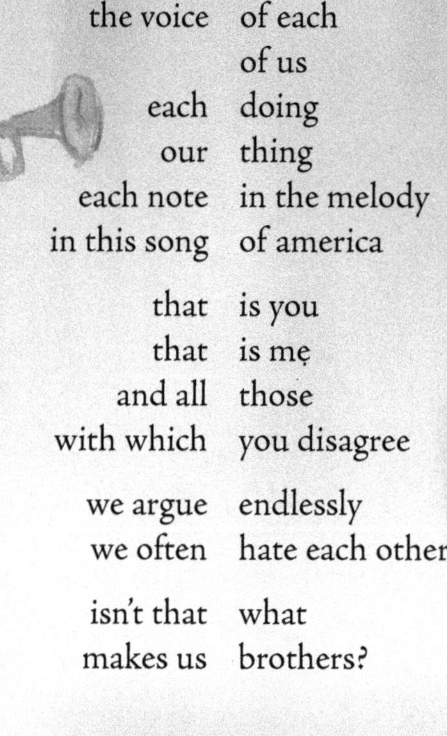

the voice   of each
            of us
each   doing
our   thing
each note   in the melody
in this song   of america

that   is you
that   is me
and all   those
with which   you disagree

we argue   endlessly
we often   hate each other

isn't that   what
makes us   brothers?

do you argue
or do you sing?

we sing
in hope of being
in being heard
in this need
to be ourselves

donne said no man
is an island
and so it follows
a song should never
be sung alone

music was never meant
for isolation
your voice is
what awakens

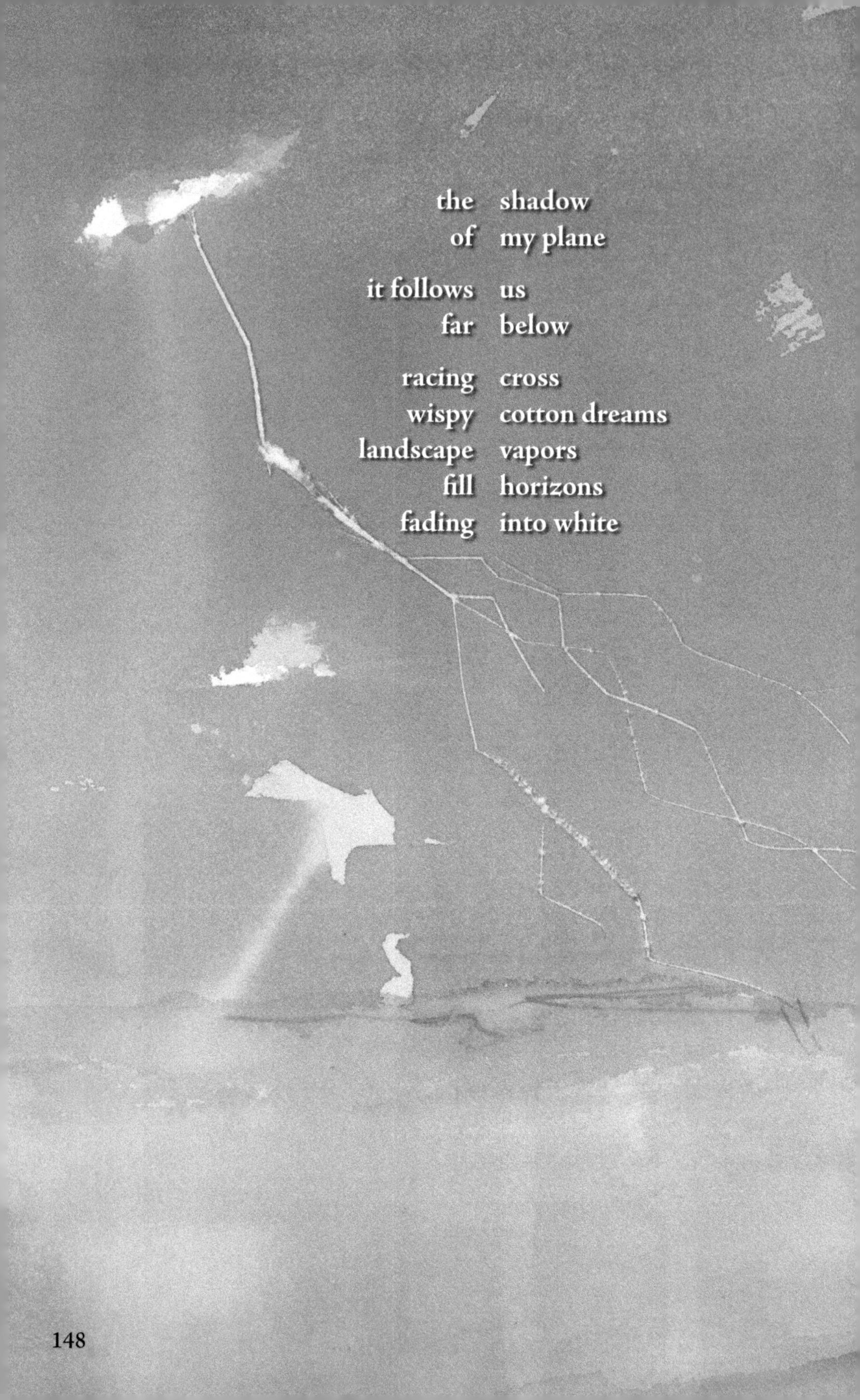

the   shadow
of   my plane

it follows   us
far   below

racing   cross
wispy   cotton dreams
landscape   vapors
fill   horizons
fading   into white

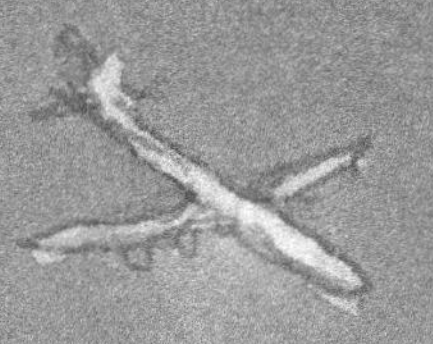

until   arising
against   our path
the song   of thunder
this lord   of the sky

such   energy

such static electricity

the bringer of storms
their   regal rain
upon   this earth

we   collide

all   the world
becomes   this cloud

we fly   inside
this storm outside

nothing is black and white

colors   fade

teams   lose meaning

the plane   is shaking

I no   longer see
red   or blue

my knuckles white

all   I see
flying   thru
this   cloud

the ephemeral   passing

away

to   this

ever

darker

shade

of gray

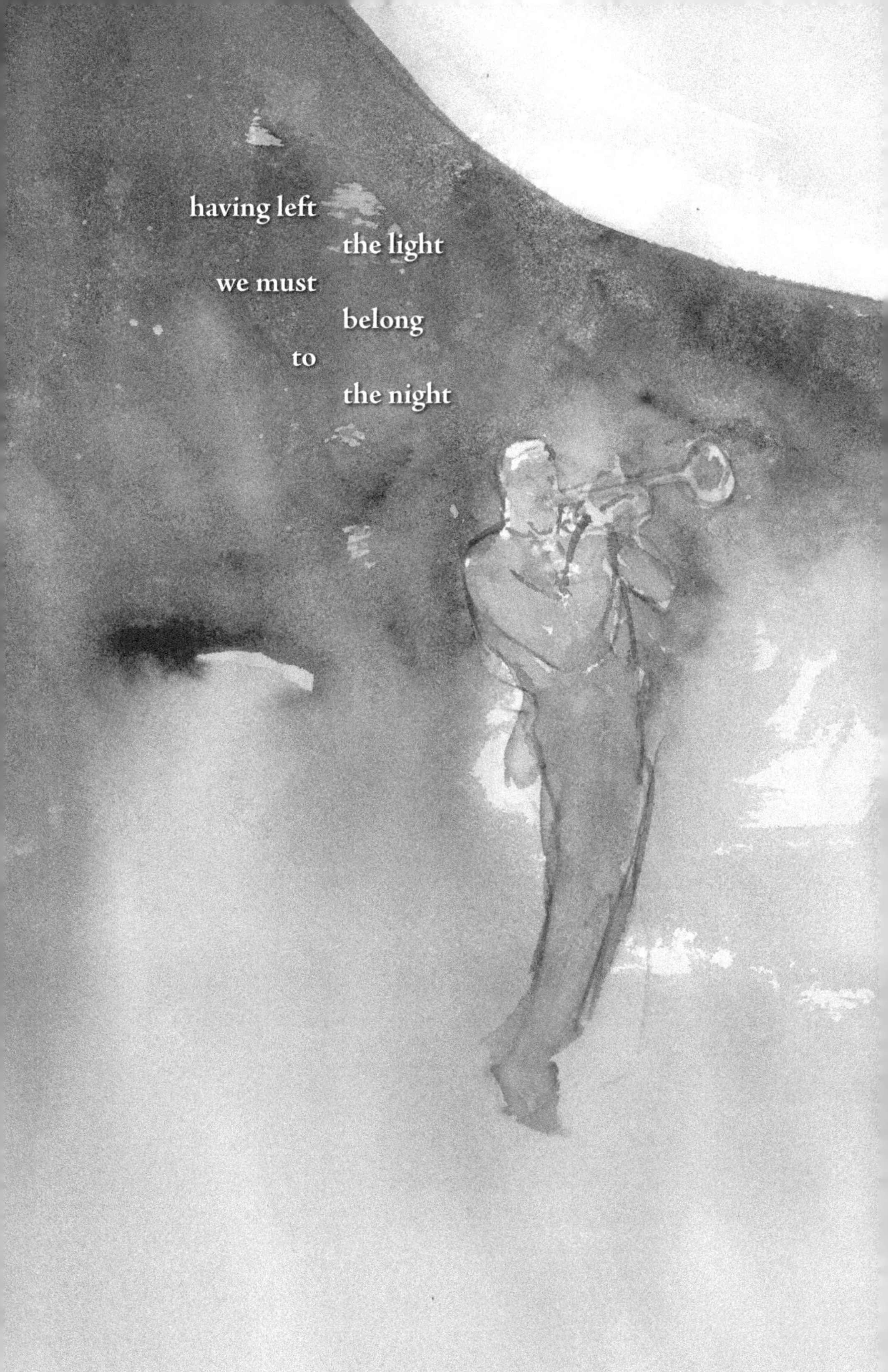

having left
the light
we must
belong
to
the night

I sit   in this
window   seat
at ten   thousand feet

we fly   into darkness
this plane   above
this   country

never   knowing
uncertainty it eats us
we feed   anxiety
has darkness finally
won   the world?

but then   my gaze
      it   falls

     not   inside
   these   cabin walls

     not   upon
    this   screen

     but   what I
  what I   actually see

outside   this window
   I see   you then
  in all   your lights
shining   against the dark

  lights   of every color
    each   a star
rebuking   darkness

these are   the lights
      of   america

your cars   your porches
the lights   above
your   streets
all these   lights of you
just doing   your thing

flood lights   over sports fields
your children   playing
little   league

headlights   speeding down
every road   and highway
ignoring each   posted limit
you believe   in every minute

I see city   skylines
the glow   of overtime
from tired   office buildings

emergency   lights
flashing red   and white
the screaming   sirens
of helpers racing   to save us

this up   all night america
with neon signs   selling
all that you   leave unspoken

spending nights   on jazz
the red glow   from dive bars
and hidden   speakeasies

that late night   dance together
where love   finds another

I see   our red
our white   and blue
but more   each of you
in pink   and purple
yellow   orange and green
a multitude of stars
twinkling in every color
all free   to be
any color   you choose

all   I see
are little   lights
not left   lights
nor right   lights

but little   kids
needing   night lights
our children   they watch us
now   so afraid
of the   dark

I see   your lights
as countless   as
the   stars

they go   on and on
for   so far
lights for   all of us
these lights   of america

stars for   each state
across a field   of blue
above stripes   of red and white
this banner   the symbol
the fabric   of america
we've sewn   together

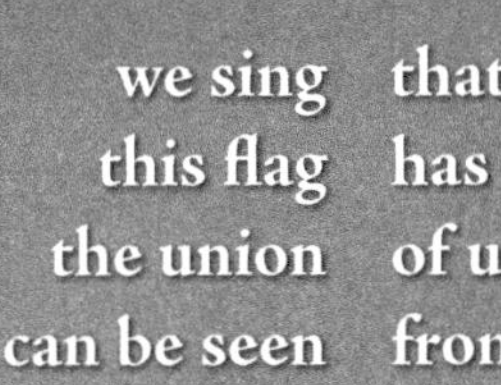

we sing   that anthem
this flag   has not fallen
the union   of us all
can be seen   from far above

each twinkle   evidence
giving truth   thru
the   night

this   we
is   america

we   the people
its light

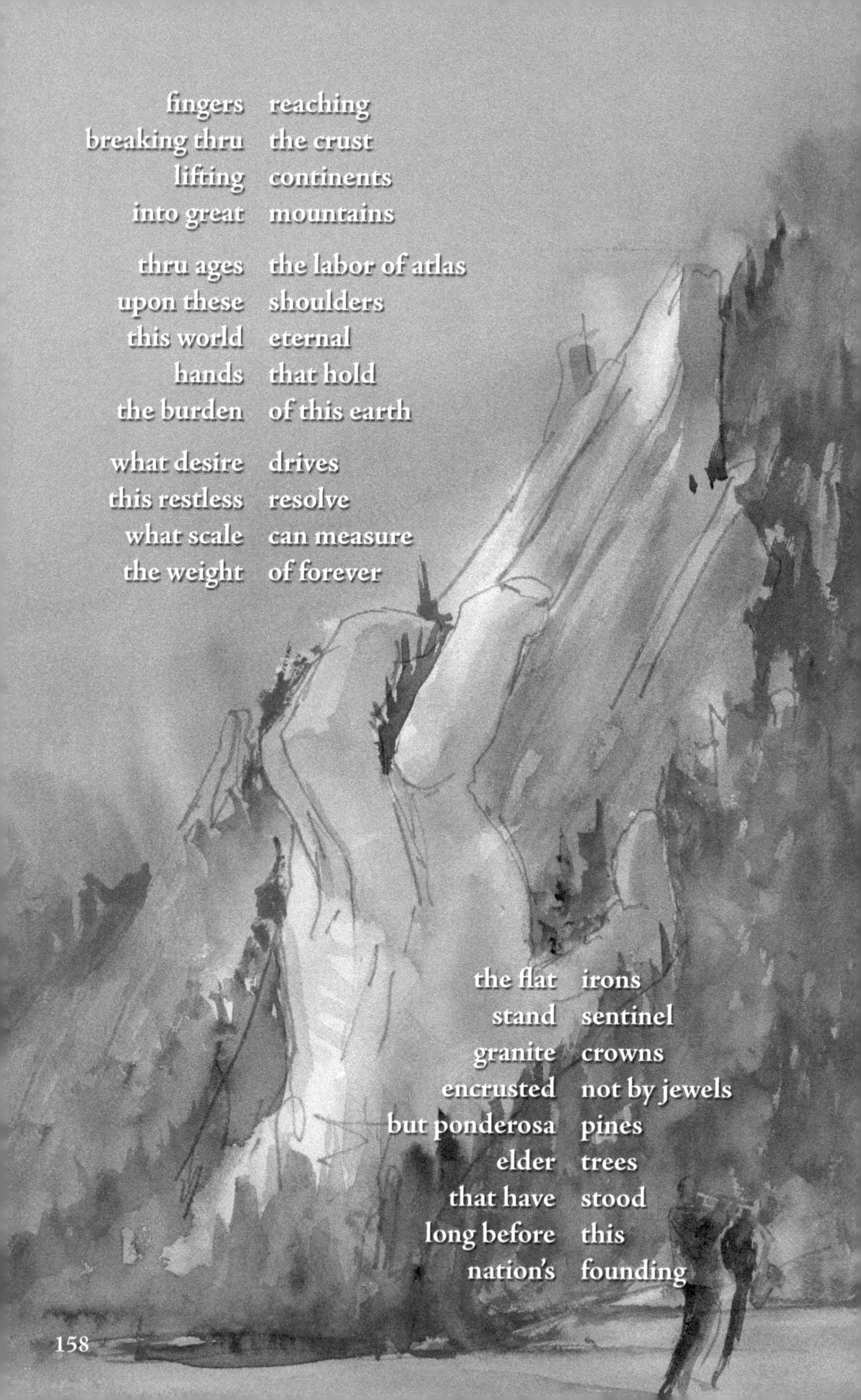

fingers reaching
breaking thru the crust
lifting continents
into great mountains

thru ages the labor of atlas
upon these shoulders
this world eternal
hands that hold
the burden of this earth

what desire drives
this restless resolve
what scale can measure
the weight of forever

the flat irons
stand sentinel
granite crowns
encrusted not by jewels
but ponderosa pines
elder trees
that have stood
long before this
nation's founding

the voices
of
the earth

the aspen   the birches
their leaves   turning gold
preparing   for the snow

they never   mind
that   they grow
amidst   the pines
they know   trees
are   trees
no matter   the color
of   their leaves

our forests   know
this   america
both   our love
of   country
and this   hate
of   color

the weight   of lives
what   hangs
from   branches

strange fruit we've hung
countless   as
the leaves   that fall

they tried   to silence jazz
to stop   the singers
holiday   still sang
that song   of sadness
until the day she died

the forest   must
bear   witness
as   we
we meet   again
the   curse
of this   nation's
               founding

it sees   our seasons
what happens   to the singers

all goodness   hangs
in the complicity of
our   branches

to the   point
               of breaking

we

you   and me

this democracy

at   the end

of   our rope

161

I stand   at
eight   thousand feet
in the middle   of america
in these rocky   mountains
where these   fourteeners rise
to touch   the sky

here   I see
this land   this country
as god   made it

without   the maps

without   the lines

to the   east
the great   plains
the endless   grass
sweeping   horizons
the farmland   that
feeds   the world

to the   west
these rugged   mountains
granite fingers   that refuse
the bite   of time

this is   our
nation's   middle
the continental   divide

this divide   is
        not   division
        but   our nation's
              spine

in difference   we come
                together
we buttress   each other

    we are   damned
  by this   division

      our   problems
 never in   our differences

  but in   that decision

I walk   this trail
on the   forest's edge
the trail   between
life   and death

to my   right
rises   a forest
roots   reaching
into   solid rock
this wall   of trees
girds   my path

to my   left
nothing
a sheer   cliff wall
tempting me to fall
into this   unknown
into the   mystery
            below

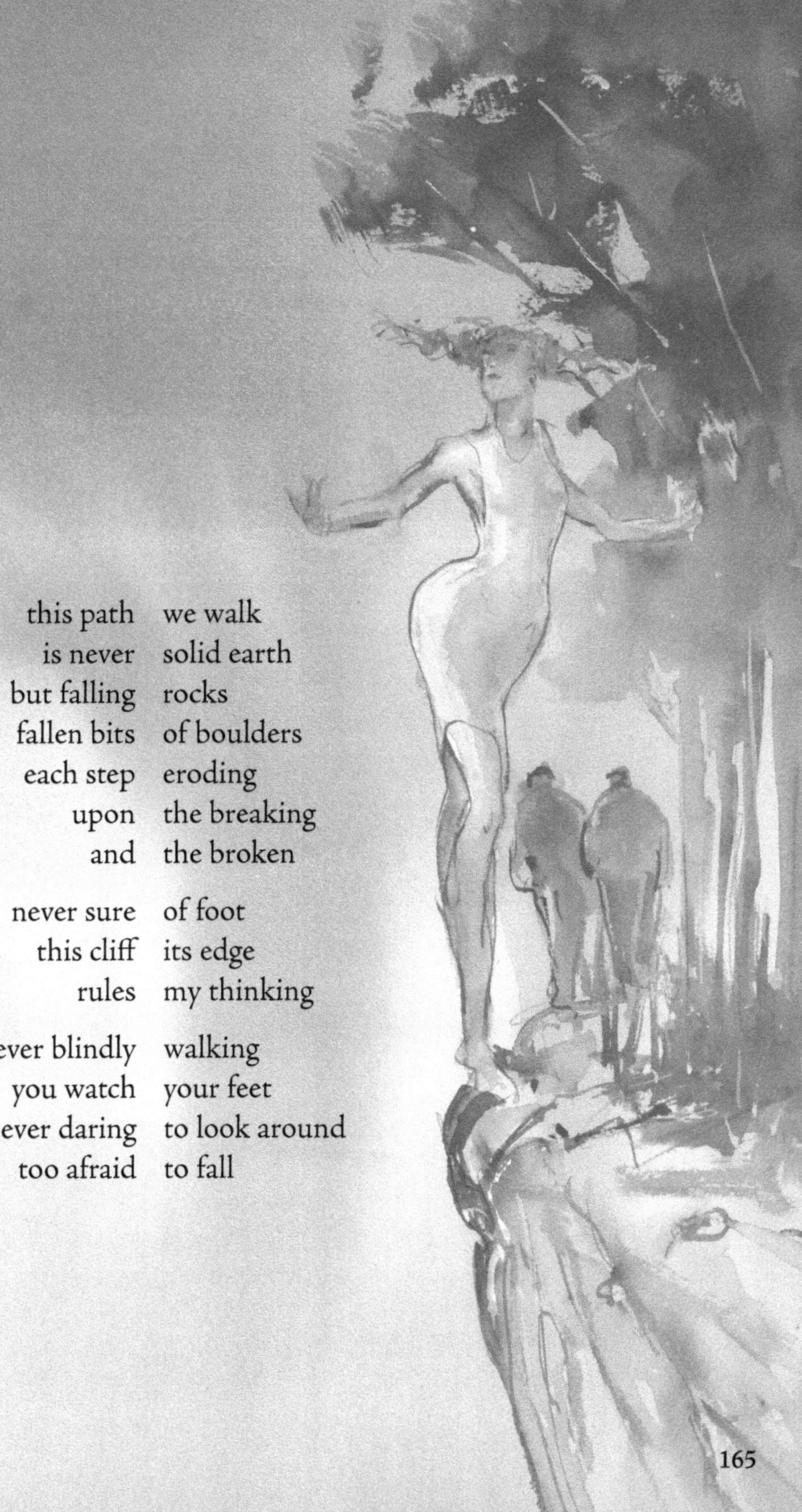

this path   we walk
is never   solid earth
but falling   rocks
fallen bits   of boulders
each step   eroding
upon   the breaking
and   the broken

never sure   of foot
this cliff   its edge
rules   my thinking

ever blindly   walking
you watch   your feet
never daring   to look around
too afraid   to fall

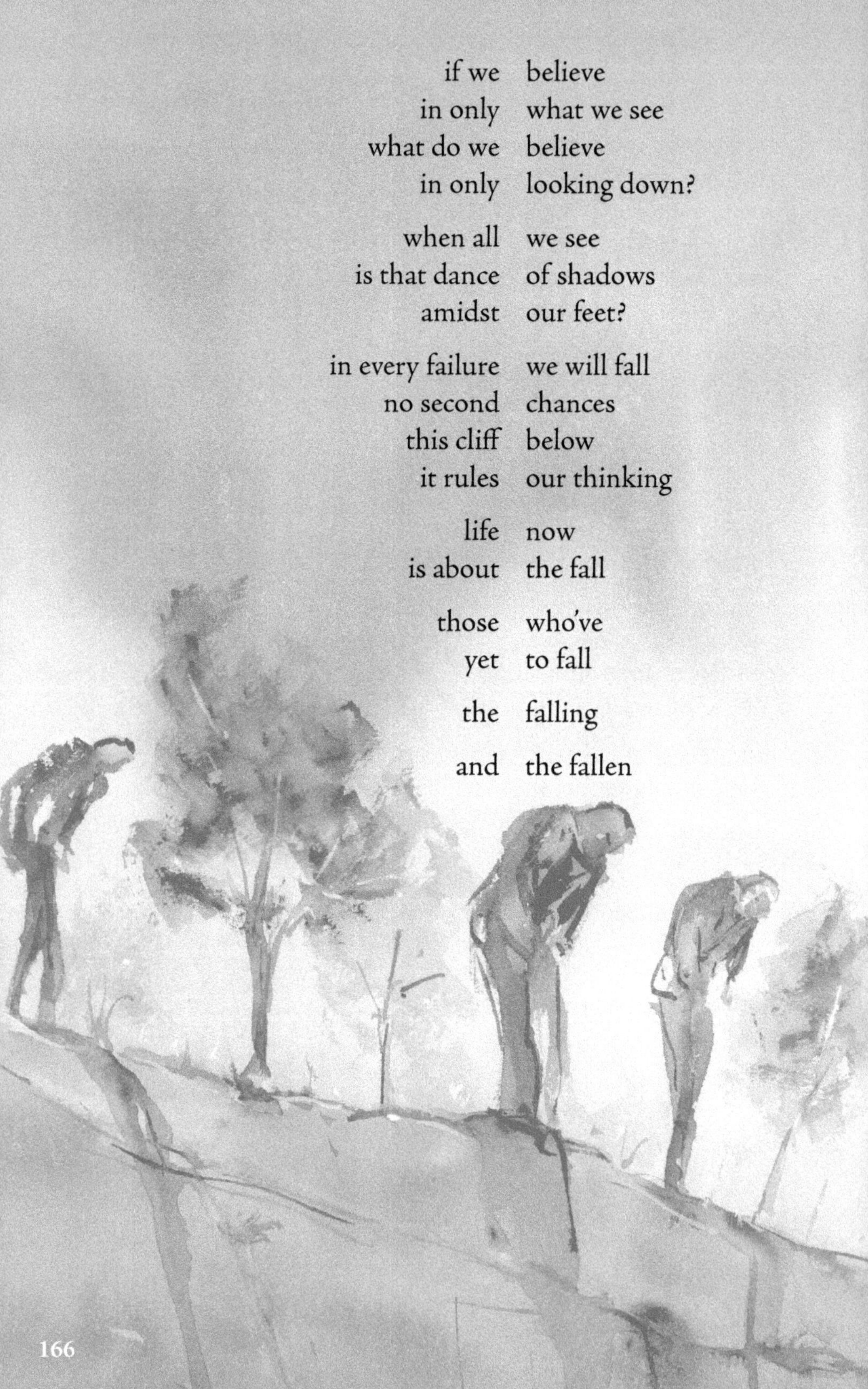

if we   believe
in only   what we see
what do we believe
in only   looking down?

when all   we see
is that dance of shadows
amidst   our feet?

in every failure we will fall
no second chances
this cliff below
it rules   our thinking

life   now
is about   the fall

those   who've
yet   to fall

the   falling
and   the fallen

the believer believes
in looking down
in what they have
always done

in endless routine
the ritual of living
never seeing never feeling
but still they wonder why
this life is never different

to ask where
where will this trail go?
where am I walking?
what is my meaning?
we walk thru life
and never know

the chains of comfort
what holds us here
are forged of repetition

this
what plato
in his lesson

must be
saw
of the cave

these shadows
upon his
of

dance
philosophy
reason

he set
from these
of

himself free
chains
blind belief

with eyes
but still
still
by

that saw
looking down
grounded
these feet

the cave was just

what you see

what you feel
from the corners of
your eyes

as knowing
is imprisoned
inside imagination

while the outside
of me
is never
fully seen

in looking down
you never
see
the sky above

169

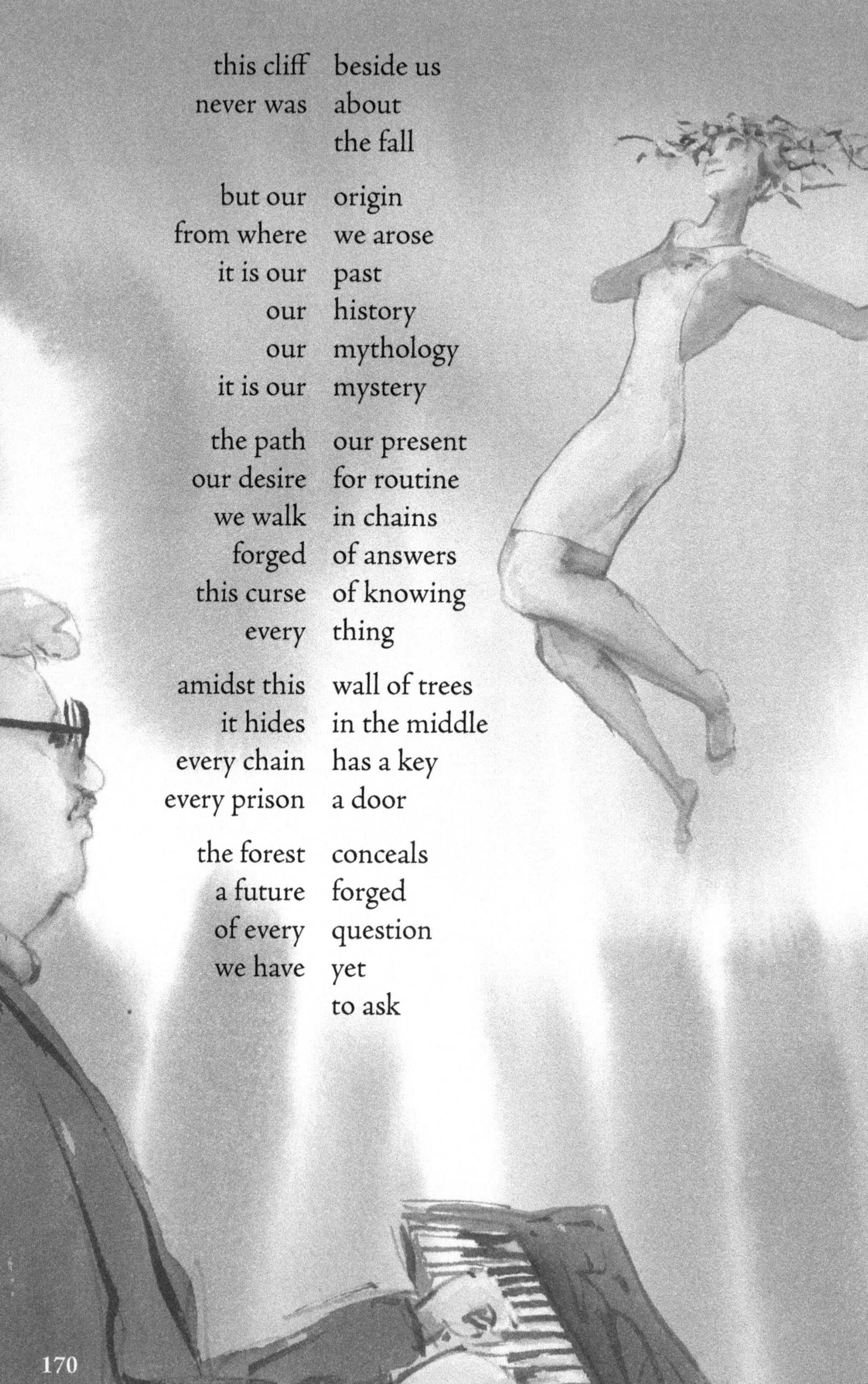

this cliff   beside us
never was   about
              the fall

but our   origin
from where   we arose
it is our   past
our   history
our   mythology
it is our   mystery

the path   our present
our desire   for routine
we walk   in chains
forged   of answers
this curse   of knowing
every   thing

amidst this   wall of trees
it hides   in the middle
every chain   has a key
every prison a door

the forest   conceals
a future   forged
of every   question
we have   yet
              to ask

the prophets   have spoken
to what   must be
                 awoken

sit   and meditate
or climb   a tree
the wonder   that is
the   spirit
this life   it happens
despite   distraction

stop this   looking down
stop   and listen
to these   birds
who sing   the songs
to greet   the dawn

just look up   to see
the sky   above
chase the   remnants
of   the rainbow

see what   comes after
after   the rain
has fed   the weeds
feel the wet   earth smell

from the   seeds
we   sow
the future   flows

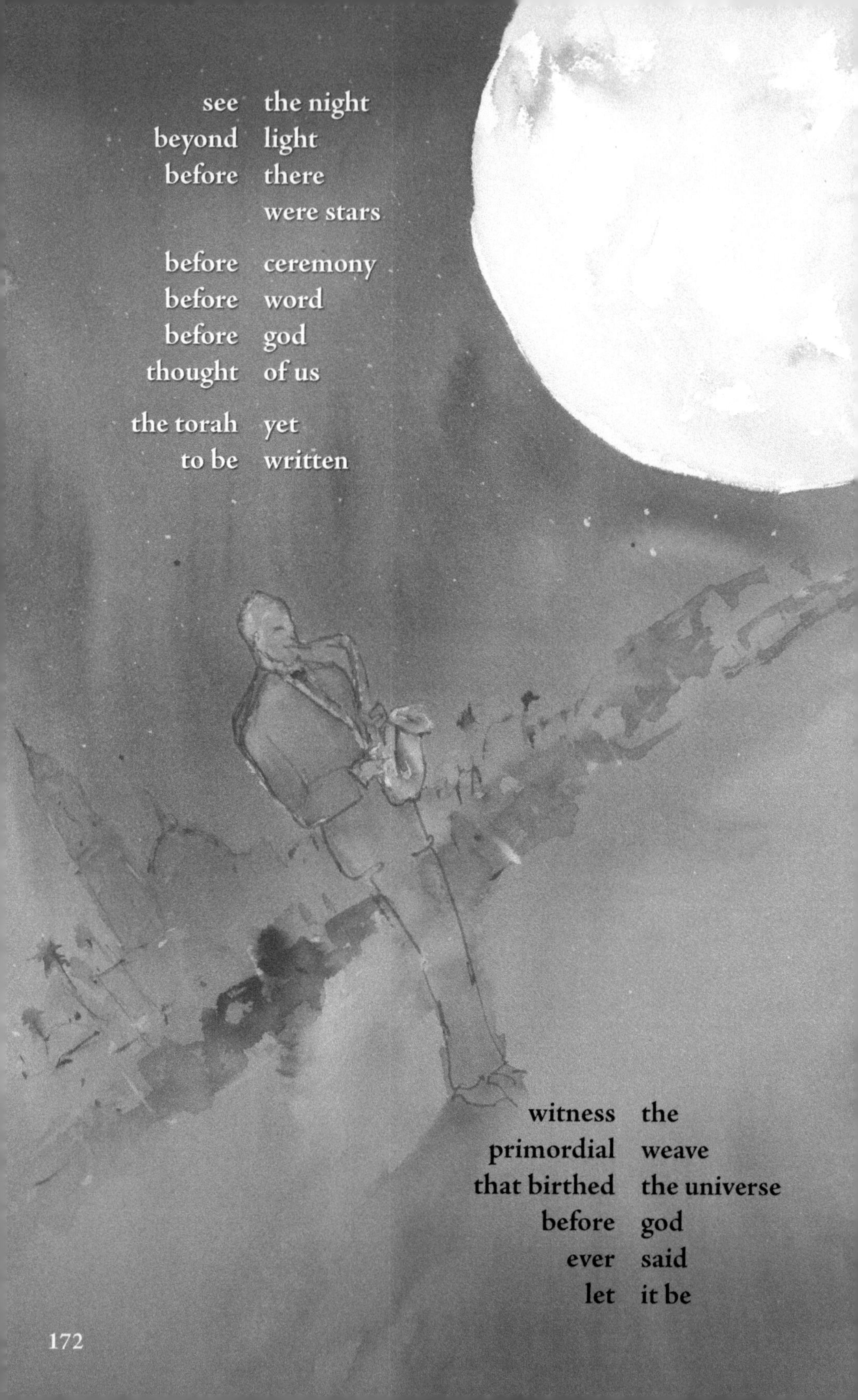

see   the night
beyond   light
before   there
         were stars

before   ceremony
before   word
before   god
thought of us

the torah   yet
to be   written

witness   the
primordial   weave
that birthed the universe
before   god
ever   said
let   it be

sleep   in that sea
learn   the lessons
that come   when
         we dream
life's   only
         certainty
will be   this
         mystery

the moon   will rise
it will   awaken tides
these tides   that pull us round
that drive us   thru our lives

this gravity
we presume   is love
in each ending   and this ending
we serve   our destiny

breathe

ya gotta
if you
ya gotta
to hit those

are to sing
listen close
notes above

the modern
made not
nor
but by
by
refusing
in having
our refusal
the side

world
by god
nature
us
humanity
to sing
to be right
to err on
of love

tree burns
upon the smoke
the song
we choke
as the world
upon
depend
that we
we've forgotten   this
breathe
we
this   is how
crowned
with leaves
amongst
these trees

in the truth
I meet
the end of song
of trees

that song
echoes
above
to the beat
the song
the forest
listen
this is
is
your
rhythm
in weeds
it hides
all around
we need
the truth
is still
round
this paradise
I talk   in circles

we remade   the garden
into   its grave
this earth   is eden
we never   left

creation
we remade   our world
we remade
all   our progress
just   breaking
babel's   curse
we need   our towers
despite   the trees
to spite   our selves
concrete   never feel
steel   and
we need
what we can

finis

postface

Where did this come from? Where did *she* come from?

She appeared in my paintings, first as a muse, a figure dancing behind the musicians, expressing that feeling of the moment. I often dressed her like Josephine Baker, that icon of the Jazz Age in her yellow banana skirt.

But then I wrote a poem about how jazz made me feel. No matter how hard life is, no matter what you are feeling, you feel the song. Your heart hears the beat. Your mind obeys the melody. For a moment you forget the war of life. The music becomes medicine.

One line in that poem described the girl with the sideways hair, which I realized, was describing this girl in my paintings. It wasn't that she came from my writing or my art, she was always there, hidden in front of me, part of my nature. As I wrote these poems I was painting to live music each night. At jazz jams and dive bars, this figure kept finding me.

The clothes she wore—what I dressed her in—these were my fear, what would people think of me.

As I wrote I realized that this, this was Eve, the first woman, an ideal that was less than real. The mortal who stole from God the apple, that gift of fire, the knowledge of good and evil, the blame for our fall. A rib made of my flesh, a dream made of myth and loneliness. My hope, this girl, made just for me.

But she was also mother nature, in all it's wildness, the mother goddess, the nymph and dryad. The naked truth found in a midsummer night's dream. Her hair not affected by gravity, swirling around her head like stars in a galaxy.

Or perhaps a voice from inside of me, my own nature, my own self, not of loneliness—but my imagination freed, now dancing in front of me.

I have a practice of reading while walking, not just writing my poems, but speaking them. Asking, "does this sound right?" or "is this my voice?"

In my words, I was hearing something I did not yet understand. That nature improvises like all jazz, all diversity the notes in its song. We evolved to feel connected to this noise, its cycle and rhythms.

I use the word nature in its broadest sense—not just the forest and its animals, but our inner nature, our instincts and feelings.

But the writing of this song made me hear its absence. We now see this world thru screens, thru devices in every pocket, our feelings driven by pervasive marketing that invades every privacy.

Artificial flavors compel our consumption. Mass produced food of empty calories that will never sate us. Alcohol and drugs to feel less, while escaping into television and video games. This economy no longer exchanges of need, but attention.

Machines now choose our words, their thoughtless generation branded as intelligence. The voices of singers have been auto-tuned into a perfection that cannot be real. The natural no longer heard, nor each other, not even ourselves—only this world we've made. The earthly city and its towers, never the garden made for us.

So fragile, so emotionally blind, so triggered by the world's jagged edges we need warnings to avoid the discomfort of anything too real. We fall into conspiracy, delusion, and disconnection. So disembodied, we must question reality. Our asking "Is this a simulation?" is a symptom.

Nietzsche's philosophy posed a central question: what becomes of ethics if we no longer believe in God. But what matters ethics when truth is dead? When we become a mob comforted by mass delusion? When we cannot discern what is real?

As an artist I engage in the practice of art. In every drawing I test myself, "do I see the world accurately?" Every error proof of my own bias. Through repetition, I drive out the redundant, the contrived, the conditioned, the artificial. I write to test my thinking.

The extremist in contrast seeks simple answers and absolute ideals. The untested utopias that drive them, are rejections of nuance and difference. One truth so perfect, so true, so certain, that any disagreement—any who disagree—must be enemies. Such conviction feeds violence, terrorism and war. The pursuit of ideals at any cost has ever led to hell on earth.

Art embraces complexity and ambiguity. Every painting, shades of gray composing contradiction. Every light argues with darkness. Every note needs silence to be heard. Art itself isn't real; its substance and clarity arise from how the artist sees, the realness of their voice.

Our eyes were only made to see light. We have chosen to see darkness.

Our ears still hear, they still serve our beating heart. If we listen, we can still hear the song. The answer has been around us all along. The song of nature is the song of creation. All existence, an echo of the voice of God.

God never said "let there be darkness," but said "let there be light."

about the author

Brian Meyer is a plein air poet and painter in jazz known for creating on the spot at local concerts and clubs in his native San Diego. His words and art arise from these moments; a practice based on jazz improvisation, developing chops outside of any comfort zone, and always asking, does this swing?

A member of the San Diego Watercolor Society, where he displays his art, and a regular at monthly paint-outs for over 10 years. These are led by Lorri Lynch on the second Saturday of each month. As Lorri always says, "If you don't go, you don't grow."

His art is about the community, and you will find him out and about in San Diego working plein air at the beach, trying to "catch" some waves in a painting, in Hillcrest at a coffee shop sketching and writing, or up in Laguna Mountains painting trees.

Many know him for being handed "random acts of art", a sketch of people just being themselves, because art matters, because being seen matters,

Brian is a US Army Veteran. He served in Desert Storm as a combat signaler for 16th Corps Support Group.

You can follow my Art at:
https://brianmeyer.DivergeISay.com/

follow my Substack at
https://artbybrianmeyer.substack.com

My Books
https://amazon.com/author/artbybrianmeyer

My Social
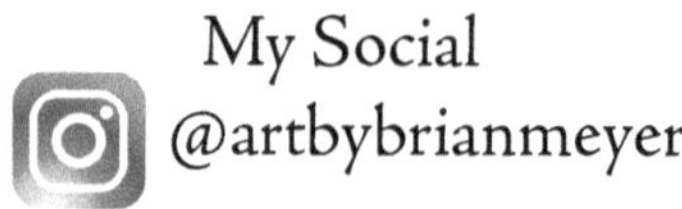
@artbybrianmeyer

and contact me directly at
brian@DivergeISay.com

calendar

I am a regular at the following San Diego locations every month, reading poems, sketching and painting watercolors. Please join me. Come out and support the arts, you are what keeps jazz alive.

Mondays	7:30pm	Monday Jazz Jam at Charades Speakeasy Inside the Balboa Bar and Grill
Tuesdays	9:00pm	Clifford and Friends (Jazz/Soul/R&B) Prohibition (Downtown San Diego)
Wednesdays	6:30pm	The Jam Session at Panama 66 Panama 66 (San Diego Museum of Art)
Sundays	5:00pm	Sunday Night Jazz Tio Leo's (Morena San Diego)
1st Friday	3:00pm	Poetry Party Santa Fe Room, Balboa Park Club
1st Friday	8:00pm	The Gravities (Soul/Funk) Whiskey Girl (Downtown San Diego)
1st Saturday	7:00pm	The Gravities Hotel Republic San Diego
2nd Thursday	9:00pm	The Gravities Seven Grand San Diego (North Park)
2nd Friday	9:00pm	The Gravities Patricks Gaslamp Pub
2nd Saturday	9:00am	Monthly Paintout San Diego Watercolor Society
2nd Sunday	3:00pm	Jihmye Poetry Spacebar Cafe & Wine Bistro
4th Thursday	7:00pm	Palabra (Poetry) Bread and Salt (Barrio Logan)
Last Sunday	2:00pm	Poets at the Grove Cypress Picnic Area (Balboa Park)

To find more live jazz follow @jazzinsandiego, a curated listing of live jazz music in San Diego for any given day of the week.

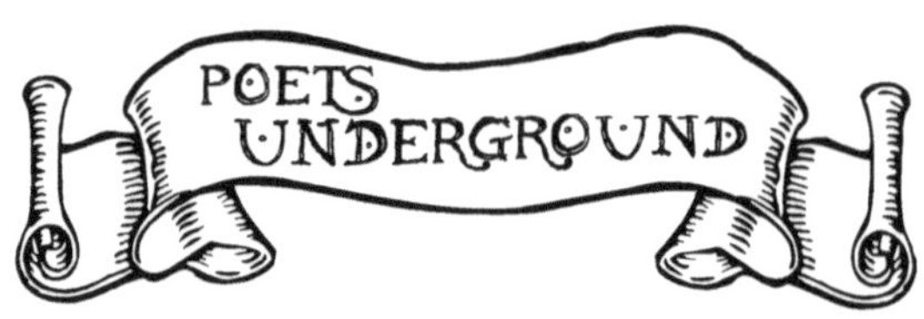

On Tuesday nights the Acid Vault hosted Poet's Underground, a spoken word community led by Sunny Rey, where Brian both regularly performed poems and painted watercolors. His first headliner as a poet was in September 2023, shortly before Modbom closed permanently that November, ending the Acid Vault.

Poets Underground continued at Template, at Queen Bee's, in local schools and in veterans outreach programs. Their goal was not just to entertain, but to elevate voices, spark creativity, and promote mental wellness.

To see so many people get on stage who had never read a poem out loud before, who continued, returning week by week, to grow and find their voice. This is the transformative power of poetry, where everyone in the community was becoming more.

Poetry is for everyone, and by creating a welcoming space, an inclusive space free of judgment, it allows poetry to develop and grow, where you can be safe to take risks, to become yourself.

Each poet was reading poems describing pain, mental illness, their own personal politics, their own personal story. All topics ripe for disagreement, but the focus was not on whether you were right, but whether you moved people. This was about community, about people with diverse views coming together, becoming family. A role model for how our wider politics could be.

Poetry Heals - Poets Underground is a movement.
Open Mics • Anthologies • Workshops

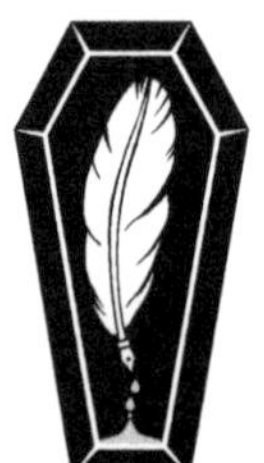

Join Us Today!

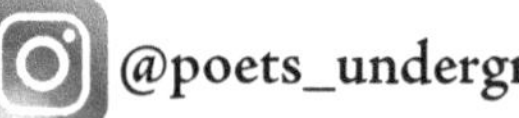 @poets_underground_

poetsundergroundsubmissions@gmail.com

www.poetsundergroundpress.com

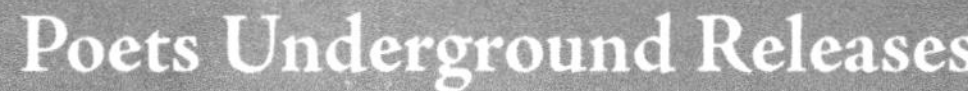

Poets Underground Releases

Poets Underground: Volume One
Anthology

Poets Underground: Volume Two: Still Here
Anthology

Through Time and Space
by Chy Cox

The Ink that Bleeds
by Anthony Azzarito

The Throw Aways
by Sunny Rey

Fuck Isolation: A Tribute to
the COVID-19 Experience
By Sunny Rey

Rot
By Sunny Rey

Quotes and Poems by a Nobody
By Sunny Rey

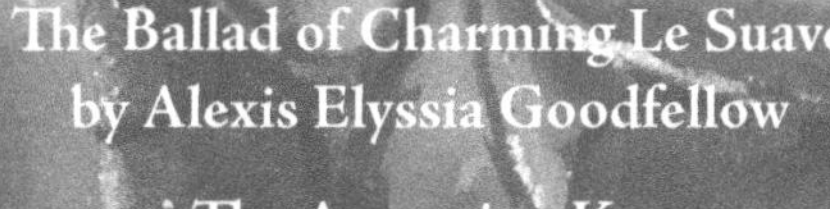

The Ballad of Charming Le Suave
by Alexis Elyssia Goodfellow

The Ascension Key
By Dennis Young Jr.

Skydiving without a Parachute
and other Success Stories
by Brooke Gerbers

Use Your Smartphone
to Shop for
Books Here

acknowledgments

Thank you to Gilbert Castellanos, for leading and curating the jam where I found my artistic voice. The month of this book's release marks ten years playing at his jam every Wednesday. For Panama 66 which made the jam possible, and always supported us every week. And to those in the local jazz community who were role models of what jazz means, such as Bob Boss, Clifford Morin, Bill Caballero, Charlie Chavez, Irving Flores, Christopher Hollyday, Carter Key, Tyler Kreutel, Joshua White, Jason Shatil, Ed Kornhauser, Leonard Patton, and so many others. Their music over ten years taught me how to improvise in watercolor to live jazz.

Thank you to the San Diego Museum of Art for hosting the weekly jazz jam there, the creative space where so many of these pictures and poems originated. A museum that does not just celebrate past masters, but living artists as well.

Thanks to the Balboa Bar and Grill, and Charades Speakeasy, and all those at the Monday Jazz Jam, led by Ian Harland, Louis Valenzuela.

And thanks to the Poet's Underground community where I developed my poetic voice, to Sunny Rey and Anthony Azzarito, and to regulars like Chris Vannoy, Chris Earnest Nelson, Olivia Mercedes, Bear Wolf, Leah Meihaus, Dennis Young.

Appreciation to the Saturday Sontage, the poetry reading group I am part of, and the Hillcrest Knox Library which hosts it. This group was formed by Curran Jeffry who passed away in 2023, now led by Charlie Berigan and its members, Susan D. Walter, Jon Von Erb, Irene Grumman, Mark Ardagna, Mary Lyons, and Michael Turner Ortega who all gave invaluable feedback on so many of my poems. I hope we live up to the values of poetry that Curran instilled in us.

And thanks to Wendy Schneider for listening to my raw poems, for setting the standard for what good writing is, that it's about having your own voice, and that even good writing gets better with editing.

I am grateful to Riston Diggs for reading my book in progress, and to Sunny Earley whose insightful feedback was instrumental in shaping the flow and overall structure of this book. And to Jesse Cunningham for his last minute line edits.

Wednesday Night Jazz Jam

Brian Meyer has been painting every Wednesday at The Jazz Session at Panama 66 starting in December of 2015. This is the jam hosted by Gilbert Castellanos inside the San Diego Museum of Art in Balboa Park. Located in the Sculpture Garden and the Panama 66 restaurant from 6:30 to 10:00 pm every week. This is his primary practice of art, where he found his voice, where he grew from just painting jazz as a subject, to learning to improvise with the music, to think like a jazz musician, to be called a member of the band. You are invited.

The best teacher is always nature herself; the second-best teacher is jazz.

This is where many of the illustrations and poems in this book originated. It is like everyone in the jam gets in sync, more creative, we feed off each other's energy, being both inspired and inspiring each other.

His first spoken word performance was at this jam, with John Murray on bass; the acclaimed young musician had never played for spoken word before. Gilbert said, "just play something funky" and John started playing Seven Nation Army.

https://www.panama66.com

Charades Speakeasy

Charades Speakeasy started in March, hidden behind a false wall at the back of the Balboa Bar and Grill. The Monday Jazz Jam starts there every week at 7:30 pm, led by Ian Harland and with regulars Louis Valenzuela, and John Opferkuch.

https://www.charadespeakeasy.com

Prohibition

Prohibition is hidden on 5th in the historic Gaslamp behind the door of a law office. It's a 20's era bar evoking that era when drinking was outlawed, now home every Tuesday night to Clifford & Friends, with Clifford Morin, Carter Key, Rashaad Graham, and Raúl Garduño. Music is from 9:00 pm until 1:00 am playing directly from the soul.

https://prohibitionsd.com

Books of my Poems

https://amazon.com/author/artbybrianmeyer

Towers Between

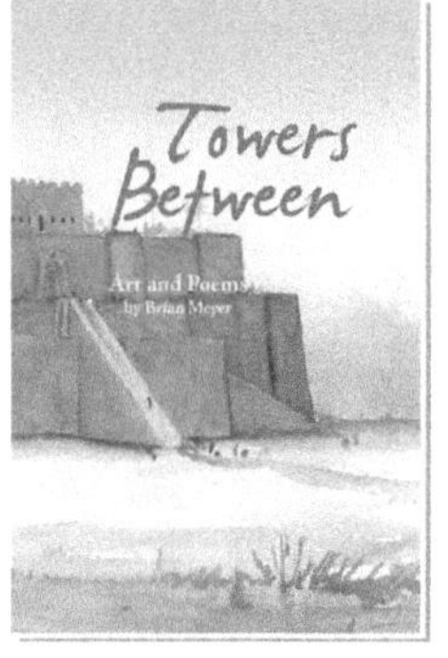

July
2016

The Politics of Hell

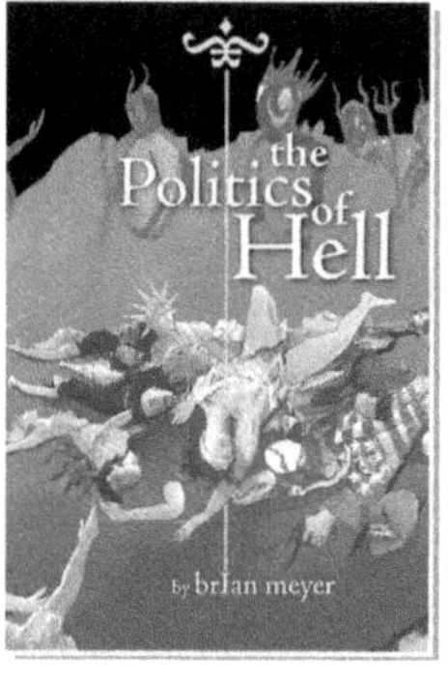

October
2024

Heart of the City
Anthology

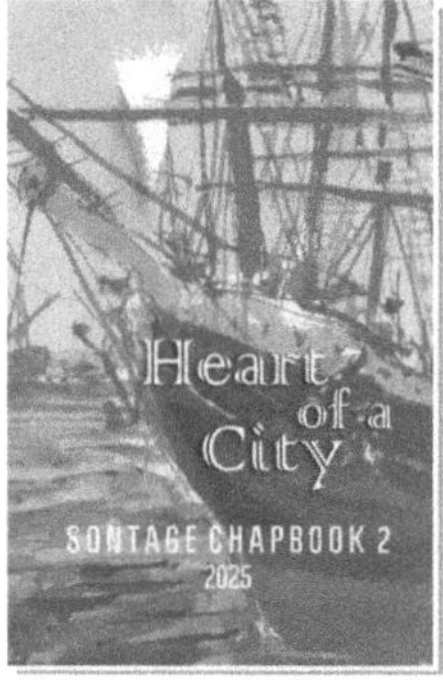

July
2016

Resistance isn't Poetry

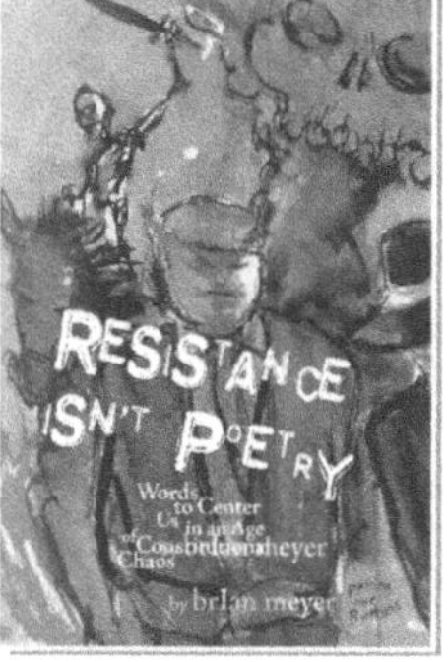

October
2024

Direct Download

The Song of the Forest

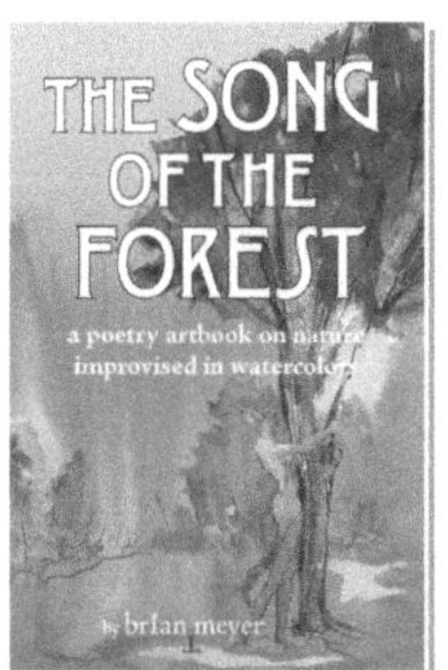

March
2026

Paintings in Jazz

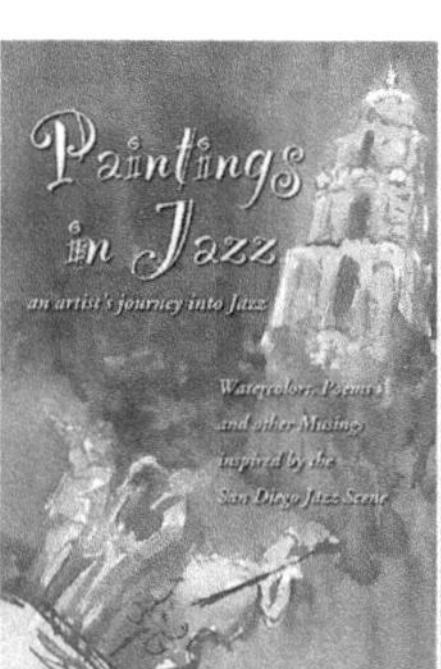

**Coming
2026**

Releases by Local San Diego Poets

San Diego Poetry Annual
Anthology

2023 is an Incorrigible Slut
by Leah Meihaus

Anything for a Dull Moment
by Michael Klam

Word Tornadoes: A Poet's Journey
by Propaganda Poet (BearWolf.PoetAF)

2020 D//Vision
by Propaganda Poet (BearWolf.PoetAF)

Some Wonder
by Eric Nelson

Holding Hands with Reality
by Curran Jeffery

What is Beat?
by Chris Vannoy

3rd & Orange
by Joshua Peralta

Equally Strange, Beautifully Different
by Gill Sotu

Harvest
by Chris Earnest Nelson

Releases by Local San Diego Musicians

Espérame en el Cielo - Album
by Gilbert Castellanos - 2022

Dialogue - Album
by Christopher Hollyday - 2020

Behind Bars - Album
by Ian Harland - 2026

It's hard for books to get noticed
these days. Whether you liked this
book or not, please consider writing
a review.

I will read every review.

Thank you.

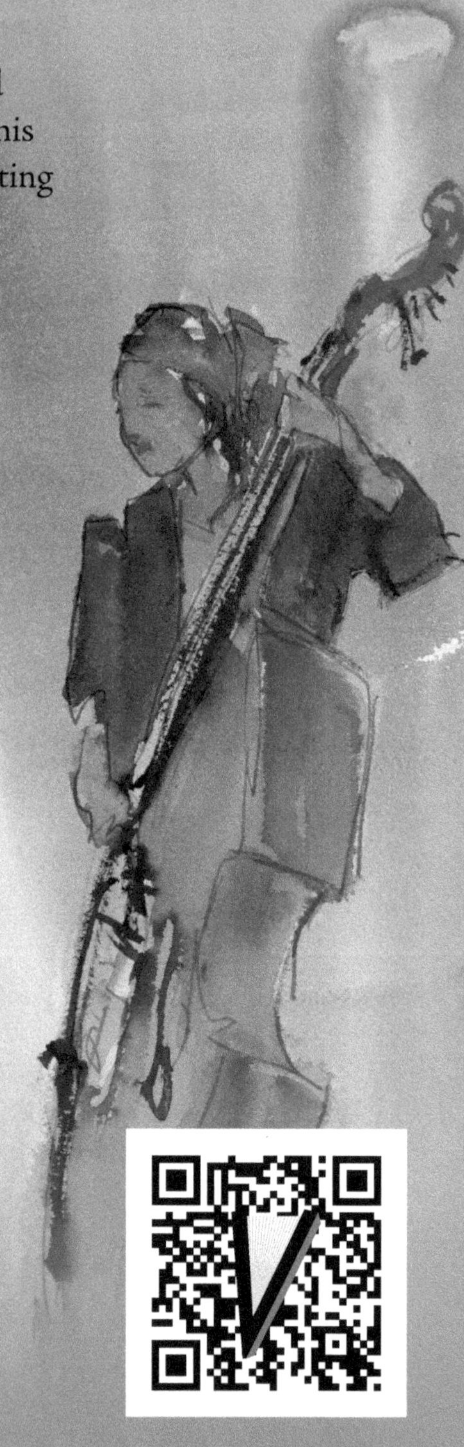

diVerge
I
SaY

Diverge I Say is my vision of how
technology and art, community
and the Internet can come together,
a website by artists for artists, a
publisher for divergent thinkers.

www.DivergeISay.com

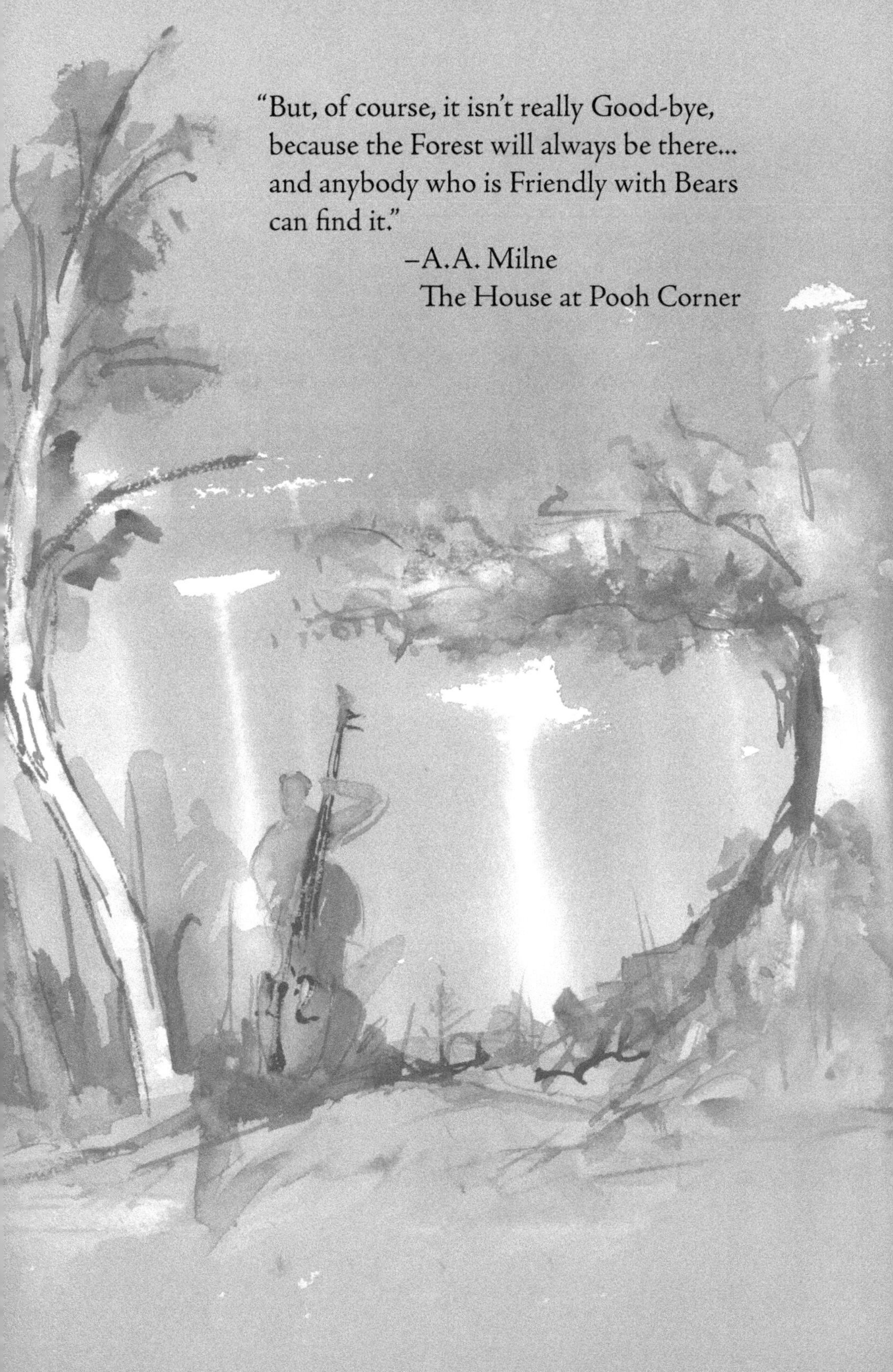
"But, of course, it isn't really Good-bye,
because the Forest will always be there...
and anybody who is Friendly with Bears
can find it."
–A.A. Milne
The House at Pooh Corner

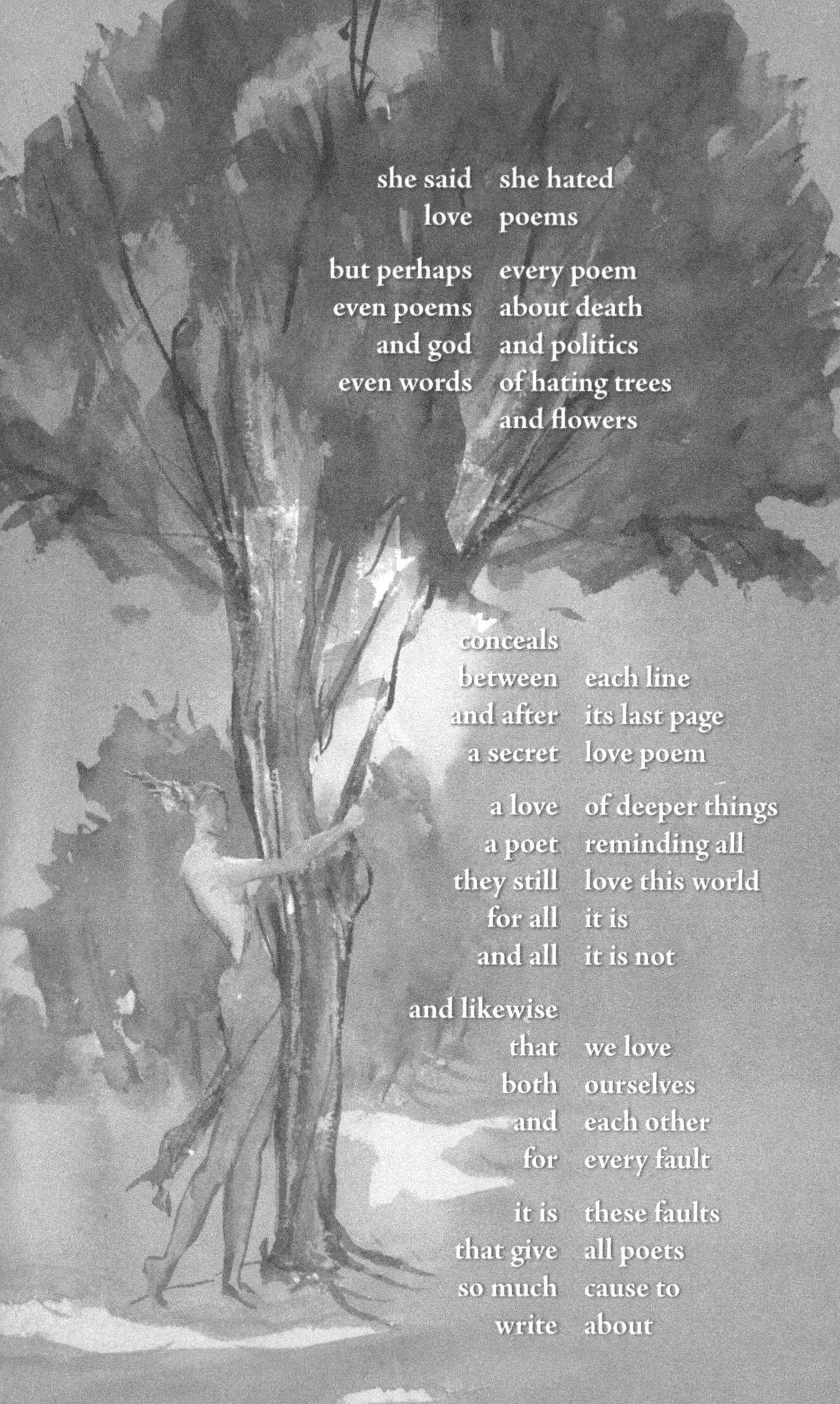
she said   she hated
love   poems

but perhaps   every poem
even poems   about death
and god   and politics
even words   of hating trees
and flowers

conceals
between   each line
and after   its last page
a secret   love poem

a love   of deeper things
a poet   reminding all
they still   love this world
for all   it is
and all   it is not

and likewise
that   we love
both   ourselves
and   each other
for   every fault

it is   these faults
that give   all poets
so much   cause to
write   about